# GOLD GOBLET COLLECTION
# 300 THREE-LINE POEMS BY XU YINGCAI

# 金爵集
## 徐英才三行诗300首

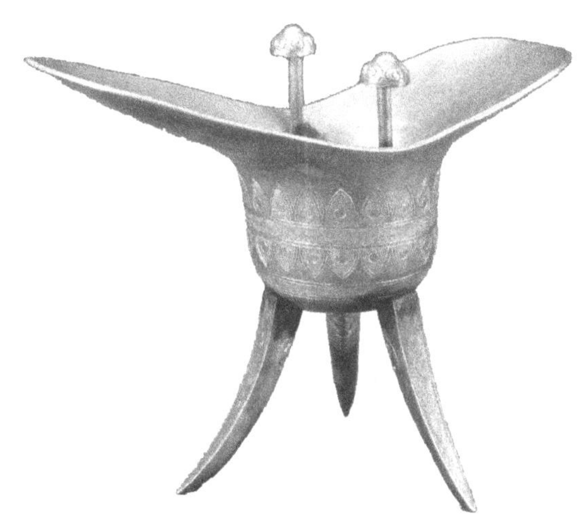

作者与翻译：徐英才
AUTHOR & TR. XU YINGCAI

CHICAGO ACADEMIC PRESS

GOLD GOBLET COLLECTION
300 THREE-LINE POEMS BY XU YINGCAI
Language: Chinese and English
Author: Xu Yingcai
Translator: Xu Yingcai
Publisher: Chicago Academic Press, Feb February 18, 2025
ISBN 978-1-965890-15-8


书　名　金爵集
　　　　徐英才三行诗 300 首
语　言　汉语、英语
作　者　徐英才
翻　译　徐英才
出版社　芝加哥学术出版社 2025 年 2 月 18 日
书　号　978-1-965890-15-8


**Library of Congress Control Number: 2025932407**


Publishing　Chicago Academic Press
　　　　　　5923 N Artesian Ave
　　　　　　Chicago IL 60659
E-mail　　　contact@chicagoacademicpress.com
Website　　http://chicagoacademicpress.com/
------------------------------------
Book Size　6X9 inches, 348 pages
First Edition February 18, 2025
------------------------------------

心窝里酿的酒

不需鼎
装入爵
醇厚、回味，飘香悠远


The Wine Brewed in My Heart

Needs no cauldron
Held in a goblet
Drifting afar with richness, aftertaste, and fragrance

亲爱的源源和泽泽：

　　谨把此三行诗诗集献给你们！这是一份语言和诗句的礼物，希望它们能启发你们、安慰你们，并在岁月中陪伴你们。愿这些诗篇成为我们共同分享的爱、喜悦与生命之美的见证。

满怀爱意
姥爷徐英才

2025年2月4日

To My Beloved Grandchildren
Blake & Peyton:

This collection is for you, a gift
of words and verses that I hope will
inspire, comfort, and stay with you
through the years. May the poetry
within these pages be a reminder of
love, joy, and the beauty of life that
we share together.

With all my love
Grandpa Yingcai Xu

February 4, 2025

# 自 序

  《中国三行诗理论与技巧》付梓以来，承蒙读者厚爱，收获诸多美誉。该书从理论建构与创作实践两个维度，对中国三行诗进行了系统性梳理，为众多三行诗爱好者提供了切实可行的创作指南。为回应读者殷切期盼，遂有本书问世，与前作相映成趣，堪称姊妹篇。若前者作为长姊，专注于三行诗的本体论与创作论；则本书可谓幼妹，重在通过丰富实例，为读者提供直观的创作范本与鉴赏路径。

  本书题名《金爵集——徐英才三行诗300首》，其命名寄托着我对三行诗的独特情钟。我常以中国古代礼器"爵"喻三行诗，两者在形制与意蕴上颇具异曲同工之妙。爵者，玲珑剔透，盛琼浆玉液，乃天子赐予诸侯之重器；三行诗则短小精悍，以简驭繁，方寸之间蕴含无限情思。佳作如佳酿，愈品愈觉醇厚绵长，余韵悠远。此中意境，已在卷首三行诗中略见端倪：

心窝里酿的酒

不需鼎
装入爵
醇厚、回味，飘香悠远

  本书辑录我近年所作三行诗凡三百首，题材包罗万象：或寄情山水，抒写天地之大美；或状物言志，描绘生灵之百态；或关注现实，记录时代之变迁。每首三行诗皆承载独特的情感密码与创作旨趣：或阐发人生至理，或营造意境之美，或刻画传神之态，或抒发幽微之情。透过这些诗作，读者自可领略三行诗艺术的多元面向与深邃内涵。

　　我独钟三行诗，实因其独特的艺术品格与时代价值。当今社会，生活节奏日益加快，人们往往疲于奔命，静心创作长篇巨制已成奢望。三行诗恰如一股清流，以其短小精悍之特质，为现代人提供了理想的诗意栖居方式。无论何时何地，皆可借三行诗抒发性灵，表达哲思。简练非简陋，短小非浅薄，三行诗往往能以最经济的语言，传递最丰富的情感，给人以无限遐思。

　　然三行诗创作实非易事。窃以为，优秀的三行诗不应止步于物象描摹，而应深入挖掘其精神内核。单纯罗列物象特征之作，往往失之平淡，盖因篇幅所限，难以铺陈细节。真正上乘的三行诗，当以简洁之语，营造张力之美，使每一行皆蕴含深意，引人深思。

　　三行诗之魅力，正在于其能以极简之形，承载至深之意。其艺术语言凝练含蓄，自成一体，既契合现代生活对简洁表达的需求，又能在诗意与哲思层面，给予读者丰盈的精神滋养。

　　《金爵集》不仅是我三行诗创作的阶段性总结，更是我对这一诗体形式长期探索与思考的结晶。愿借此书与广大读者共享三行诗的艺术之美，让更多人在短短三行之间，感受诗歌的隽永魅力与思想的深邃力量。三行诗以其独特的形式展现了诗歌创作的无限可能，愿这本《金爵集》能为您开启一扇通向诗意与哲思的大门。

徐英才

2025 年 1 月 26 日

# Preface

Since the publication of *Chinese Three-Line Poetry: Theory and Techniques*, I have been deeply grateful for the warm reception and the many kind accolades it has garnered. This work systematically explores Chinese three-line poetry from the perspectives of both theoretical foundations and creative practices, offering practical guidelines for many enthusiasts about this poetic form. In response to readers' enthusiastic anticipation, this new book has now come into being as a complementary follow-up, a sister volume to the earlier one. If the former, as the elder sister, delved into the ontological nature and creative theory of three-line poetry, then this volume, like a younger sister, focuses on offering a rich collection of examples to provide readers with intuitive templates for both creative inspiration and appreciative understanding.

The title of this book, *Gold Goblet Collection—300 Three-Line Poems by Xu Yingcai*, reflects my unique feelings toward three-line poetry. I often liken three-line poetry to the ancient Chinese ceremonial vessel known as the "goblet" (爵, jué), as both share subtle harmony in form and significance. A goblet is exquisitely crafted, luminous, and designed to hold fine wine, a precious vessel granted by the Son of Heaven to his vassals. Similarly, three-line poetry, though compact, distills vast ideas into a small, potent space. Like fine wine, a well-crafted three-line poem deepens and enriches with each savoring, leaving a lingering fragrance in the mind. The artistic essence of this idea is encapsulated in my opening poem of the book:

The Wine Brewed in My Heart

Needs no cauldron
Held in a goblet
Drifting afar with richness, aftertaste, and fragrance

This book collects 300 three-line poems I have written over recent years, spanning a wide range of themes: some express emotions through nature, painting grand portraits of the world; others describe objects and convey aspirations, illustrating the myriad forms of life;

still others capture the pulse of reality, chronicling the changes of the times. Each poem carries its own emotional depth and creative intent: some articulate profound truths about life, others craft vivid imagery, some capture poignant moments, while others express subtle emotions. Through these poems, readers can discover the diverse facets and deeper meanings of three-line poetry.

My deep affection for three-line poetry stems from its unique artistic character and contemporary relevance. In today's fast-paced society, where people are often hustling and bustling about, the opportunity to sit down and create long, intricate works is often a luxury. Three-line poetry offers a refreshing alternative, providing a perfect poetic form for modern individuals who crave both brevity and depth. Regardless of time or place, one can express profound thoughts and philosophical reflections in just three lines. Conciseness does not equate to simplicity, and brevity does not imply shallowness; three-line poetry often conveys the deepest emotions in the most economical language, leaving the reader with endless room for contemplation.

However, composing three-line poetry is no simple task. I believe that truly great three-line poems should do more than simply describe objects; they must delve into their spiritual essence. Works that merely enumerate characteristics often fall short because the limited space does not allow for full elaboration. Exceptional three-line poems employ concise language to craft both tension and beauty, making each line imbued with meaning that invites deep contemplation.

The charm of three-line poetry lies in its ability to convey profound insights with remarkable simplicity. Its succinct and subtle artistic language forms a unique system that meets the modern demand for simplicity while offering readers spiritual nourishment on both poetic and philosophical levels.

*The Gold Goblet Collection* is not only a summary of my phase of three-line poetry creation, but also the culmination of my long-term exploration and reflection on this form. It is my hope that this book will allow readers to share in the artistic beauty of three-line poetry, enabling more people to experience the enduring charm of poetry and the profound power of thought distilled into just three short lines. Three-line poetry, with its unique form, reveals infinite possibilities for poetic expression, and I trust that *The Gold Goblet Collection* will serve as a gateway for readers to enter the realm of poetic beauty and philosophical reflection.

Written and Translated by Xu Yingcai
January 26, 2025

# 前　言

## 三行世界的诗美呈现
### 《金爵集——徐英才三行诗三百首》

诗歌之美，其美无穷，比如思想的丰美、情感的真美、诗味的醇美、语言的精美、想象的瑰美、意境的隽美、创意的奇美、节奏的唯美、形式的优美等等。写诗，是诗美创造的探索之旅；品诗，是诗美享受的精神盛宴。读《金爵集——徐英才三行诗三百首》，犹如品美酒一坛，一爵一爵令人醉美。

## 惜字如金的凝练美

诗者，简约、简练、简洁但绝不简单、简陋之体也，讲求高度凝练、精炼。朱自清就讲："诗的语言最经济，情感更丰富。"微诗，尽可能以最经济、最简练的字句表达出最丰富、最精彩的内容，以有限抒写无限，缩龙成寸，尺幅千里。

徐英才先生的三行诗就十分注重语言的凝练美，以少寓多，以小见大，简中求丰，见微知著。这正如先生所说《我的诗》："无需长江那么长/却像它那样深邃湍急/映着天空　高山　林莽……"是故，写三行诗，当"挥动心剑 / 截断冰川，推入大海/把生命的源藏在冰尖下"（《微诗》）。其诗追求简约凝练，有的甚至凝练如短剑匕首，诗锋锐利，直击人心。

如《笛》仅四个字："妙/音/横空"就把横吹笛子竖吹箫的生动形象与其美妙天籁表达得淋漓尽致，令人陶醉。如《九寨沟》："沟沟/是/勾，"只四个字一个谐音法就展现了诗人对九寨沟美景的深刻感悟和独特表达。

《朦胧诗》："云中/龙/爪，"仍然只用了短短四个字，通过一个比喻，用"云中龙爪"展现了契合该诗若隐若现特点的生动画面，又用龙在云中伸展的利爪雄姿，表现了朦胧诗这一诗歌流派批判社会、寻找光明、探求意识，关怀人文等的精神内涵。

《浪淘沙》："人/物/史，"巧妙借用了中国古诗词词牌"浪淘沙"，仅用三个字，就把"风流总被雨打风吹去"以及大浪淘沙方始见真金的主题思想表现得真真切切。

这些诗作，不仅文字简约，而且内涵丰盈，正如郑板桥所言，有着"以少少许胜多多许"的妙趣。

## 自然朴实的平淡美

诗有"气象峥嵘，五色绚烂"的华丽瑰玮之美，也有"清水出芙蓉，天然去雕饰"的朴素平淡之美。明代诗人丘浚《答友人论诗》有言："眼前景物口头语，便是诗家绝妙辞。"清代著名散文家姚鼎说："文章之境，莫佳于平淡，措语遣意，有若自然生成者。"当代大诗人艾青也认为："深厚博大的思想，通过最浅显的语言表演出来，才是最理想的诗。"

徐英才先生的三行诗，其所见所思，所感所悟，所状所抒，"寄至味于澹泊"，朴素简洁，通俗易懂，几乎无一生僻字，朴实无华，"有若自然生成"，却字字句句戳人心窝，直击灵魂深处。

比如，《花》："面朝阳光/再小/也灿烂。"平实的语言，启迪人们只要面向阳光，心怀希望，就能绽放出属于自己的美好和灿烂。《风铃》："老家带来的/每一声/都闹在心上。"平淡的叙述中，只一个"闹"字，让绵绵思乡之情跃然纸上。

当然，"看似寻常最奇崛，成如容易却艰辛。"所谓平淡之"平"，并不是平平常常，而是平中有奇的；所谓平淡之"淡"，并不是淡而无味，而是淡中见浓的。绚烂至极，归于平淡；繁华落尽，方见真纯。因而平淡之美，是一种炉火纯青的美，返朴归真的美，是诗人的艺术修养和思想修养同时成熟后，才能具有的一种气敛神藏、内蕴外朴的艺术特色。

比如，《谁把春天藏了起来》："几只小鸟／用爪／在雪地上到处扒拉，"文字的铺成与衔接简洁却紧密，场景的创设与描绘，自然却富有想象力；《母亲端来的欢笑》："热腾腾地／回响在饭桌上／萦绕全家。"自然流畅，了无痕迹，展现了幸福、温馨、和谐的场景。用宋代大诗人苏东坡的话讲，这"其实不是平淡"，乃"绚烂之极也"。

## 生动贴切的意象美

"言不尽意，立象尽之。"唐代诗评家司空图说："意象欲出，造化已奇。"意象是诗歌的基本构成要素和功能单位，是诗歌的灵魂和生命，是诗歌艺术的精灵。有意象就有诗味，无意象就无诗味。

徐英才先生三行诗的意象运用，生动贴切，匠心独具。如《长江说》："谁的剑也没我的犀利／一洪劈开／南北　温寒还有才与将。"用犀利的"剑"这一意象来比喻长江，它劈出了南北温寒的自然差异，以及"南方才子北方将"的人文特点，以夸张的手法描绘了长江的壮阔与威力。《月（二）》："一只荷包／里面装满／母亲给我讲过的童话故事。"诗中，"一只荷包"作为核心意象和承载着深厚情感与回忆的载体，展现了母爱的伟大与童年时光的纯真美好。

再比如《春雨》："竖琴／天籁轻起／大地喜形于色。"《秋色》："浓烈的黄酒／一呷／就醉。"《思念》："是一枚／插在心房里的红豆枝／汲我脉动的血日夜生长。"《夕阳》："火红的句号／句住又一个丰硕／跃向另一个辉煌。"《月牙》："是只犀角／这边是我／那边是你。"

这些诗中的"竖琴"、"黄酒"、"红豆枝"、"句号"、

"犀角"意象，皆很具体、形象、生动，发挥了营造氛围、借景抒情、引发联想、传达哲理等作用，大大增强了诗作的艺术感染力，可谓"独具之匠，窥意象而运斤"。

## 张力十足的跳跃美

文章之妙，妙在起伏。清代文人袁枚曾说"文似看山不喜平"，意思是写文章应像观赏山峰那样奇势迭出，最忌平坦。同样，诗歌因跳跃方起伏变化、波澜多姿。跳跃性是诗歌文体有别于其他文学文体的基本美学属性，无论是意义的跳跃、情绪的跳跃、诗眼的跳跃，还是语言的跳跃、意象的跳跃、节奏的跳跃，或者是时空的跳跃等等，都是诗歌获得弹性、张力、含蓄、空白等美学素质的基本手段，是诗意空间不断创生和拓展的有效策略。

正如诗人所言，《三行诗》"一行是盆/二行是植/三行是蓝天"，同样可以展现跳跃之美。徐英才先生在其专著《中国三行诗理论与技巧》中，就从创作的角度，提出了一种三段法或者叫三步一曲的内在结构，很像体育运动中的一个跳远过程：起跑（呈现对象）、踏板（具化对象）、弹跳（升华对象）——直到诗的远方。这不仅是一种结构的跳跃，更是意义的跳跃，同时也是多种技巧运用的跳跃。

比如，《白云》："飞吧，飞吧/入夜前赶到西天/能穿上霞光焰焰的袈裟。"在白云、霞光、袈裟的意象跳跃中，增加了诗歌的神秘与浪漫色彩，赋予了白云以宗教或神圣的象征意义，展示了对人生自由和美好的追求。《父亲的扁担》："已被岁月压成/沉重的拐棍/我的眼光常从它移向那根屋梁。"在扁担、拐杖、屋梁的意象跳跃中，抒写了父亲的艰辛付出和诗人心中"父爱如山"的脊梁形象。

又比如，《空椅子》："路灯几度点亮/它仍在等待/那些醉人的蜜语。"《人生》："一粒向西而飘的微尘/身不由己，不知落点，不知落时/那就飘逸吧。"《仁爱河》："我是一条船/无论急行缓淌/都行不出母亲开凿的河。"诗人的大量这类诗作，都可以说是其三行诗"三步一曲"内在结构理论的实践，都在积蓄力量中于尾句"临门一脚"，完成了诗意的升华和惊心跳跃。

## 含蓄深沉的情感美

诗歌的情感表达方式，既有如飞瀑直下豪放激昂的壮志豪情，也有如静水深流欲说还休的含蓄深沉。含蓄美是中国古典诗词普遍的艺术追求，讲求语近情遥，言近旨远，含而不露，余味绵长。刘勰《文心雕龙》就说："深文隐蔚，余味曲包。"意指文章写得深刻，便含有内在的美，包藏着味外之味。

徐英才先生的三行诗尤其是抒情诗并没有激情的汪洋恣肆、淋漓喷发，而是蕴藉含蓄，语浅情深，意味深长，在看似平常的叙述中，蕴藏着诗人浓厚的感情。

如《春曲》："晨空当纸　电缆作线/上面，一大群小鸟在摆谱/下面，村口涌出数百泥脚演奏者。"诗人以富有创意的比喻，描绘了一幅充满生机与活力的农村春日早晨画卷，抒写了对劳动者的赞美。《故乡的小路》："弯弯曲曲/每一弯　都挽着我的怀念/每一曲　都勾着我的心魂。"读来看似微波荡漾，却以质朴的语言，简洁明了的意象和深情的表达，成功地触动了读者的心弦。《并非传说》："没见过铁棒磨成针/见过母亲用数十个寒暑/磨平了衣板上的木棱。"这首诗同样情感内敛、深沉，令人怦然心动。

而诗人写父亲的三行诗，更是具有内敛隽永、蕴藉含蓄的深沉之美。如《父亲（二）》："大自然的杰作/额上的皱纹由风雕成/浑身的古铜色　太阳漆出。"《往事》："都浮雕在/父亲满掌的老茧上/难以退却。"它通过对父亲皱纹、肌肤、老茧的传神描绘，塑造了一个勤劳而感人的形象。而《父亲（三）》："一根筋/自己种地，却不让我下田/要我在文字里耕耘。"《路》："父亲走过的路/都粗犷地深刻在他的额上/

不愿遗传给我们。"《陀螺（二）》："父亲　不停地抽/每一抽/都是爱。"则在看似平静的叙述中，展现了父爱的深沉与伟大，以及天下所有父亲"望子成龙"的无限期望。

当然，隐而不露，藏而不显，贵在藏了该藏的、隐了该隐的，露了该露的、显了该显的，这是一种选择的智慧。只讲隐或藏，就会艰涩难懂；只讲露或显，就会了无诗意。隐是为了更好的露，藏是为了更好的显。关键要有味，要有诗味、情味、意味、趣味，耐人品味，要能够启迪和激发读者想象的空间。诗人当是深谙其道的。因此，我们读诗人的三行诗，就能够从诗人露或显出的情感线头，拽出隐或藏的深沉情感。

## 瞻言见貌的画面美。

"瞻言而见貌"出自刘勰的《文心雕龙·物色》，形容用语准确、生动，如同见到景物的形貌一般，这也正是古人所谓"状难写之景如在目前"。无论是中国还是西方，都有"诗画同源"说。北宋张舜民在《跋百之诗画》中更是认为："诗是无形画，画是有形诗。"古希腊抒情诗人西蒙尼蒂斯也提出："诗是有声画，犹如画是无声诗。"法国古典主义评论家拉宾说："诗中的构思，犹如画面的布局。"

徐英才先生的三行诗，只寥寥几笔，就常常给我们带来了瞻言见貌的画面美，他的诗，可以说正是"诗中有画"，栩栩如生。

比如《垂暮》："路的尽头/老人拖长的身影慢慢淡去/天边　那抹浓厚的晚霞也渐渐消隐。"这是一幅老之已至的暮年图。它通过对老人身影和晚霞的细腻描写，传达了时光流逝与生命老去的主题，充满了岁月沉淀的韵味和淡淡的哀愁，也启示我们珍惜当下，把握生命中的每一个瞬间。

《春雷》："惊醒了梦睡的蝶/她探头蛹屋外，四下张望/踏春的路。"这是一幅万物萌动的迎春图。它通过春雷唤醒蝶的意象，用拟人化的手法，生动地展现了春天的到来和万物复苏的景象，也表达了人们对春天的热爱和向往。

《夜空（二）》："一只孤雁／横过满月／破镜望重圆。"这是一幅孤雁印月图。它通过孤雁、满月、破镜等意象，传达了诗人对生活中难以避免的分离与孤独的深刻感悟，以及对团圆、完满的向往。

《犁》："父亲的背／哪一朵泥花／不是弓着身开出。"《老农》："一把锄头／硬是把太阳从东边拽到西边／然后掮着月牙下山。"这是两幅艰辛劳作的耕作图。它形象地展示了对父亲、对老农的赞美和诗人深沉浓厚的感情。

《翅膀》："左手拉着爸／右手拉着妈／我是一只会飞的鸟。"这是一幅温馨甜蜜的三人图。它成功地展现了孩子与父母之间的深厚情感以及孩子对自由飞翔的向往，不仅让人感受到家庭的温暖和亲情的力量，还激发了人们对自由、探索和成长的无限遐想。更重要的是，它让读者感受到了一个完整家庭对孩子成长的重要性。有了完整的家庭，孩子就能像诗歌所描绘的画面一样张开双翼飞翔；一个破碎的家庭，孩子就会缺少翅翼，难以自由地飞翔。

## 妙思迭出的奇异美。

奇异是诗歌最本质的特征之一，是诗歌的生命力之所在，也是诗人创造性的重要体现。这种奇异之美表现在思想挖掘上的语次崛奇或"言人之所未言"、语言运用上的奇巧奇妙和鲜活新异的"陌生化"或"反常化""奇特化"、写作角度把握上的独辟蹊径，以及表达方式等诸多方面能给人带来耳目一新的感觉。

徐英才先生的三行诗，常常平中见奇，别开生面。如《浪》："江水的／心／思。"只五个字，却简直是神来之笔。

它展现了江水渴望不断涌起大浪的特点，寓意有志者的宏伟志向，体现了诗人的内在情感与对自然界的敬畏和赞美。

《二胡独奏〈江河水〉》："一根弦是左岸　一根弦是右岸/中间咆哮的/是民族自强的呐喊。"诗人用二胡的两根弦来比喻黄河的"左岸"和"右岸"，可谓奇思妙想；而"中间咆哮的/是民族自强的呐喊"一语激荡出民族所经历过的深沉悲痛与不屈的抗争精神，诉说着民族的不息自强史与奋斗的历程。

《昙花》："睁开花的明眸/看到这世界满尘/当天就闭了。"这首诗将昙花一现别出新意，既赞美了昙花的美丽与高洁，也寓言了一种超然物外、不为世俗所累的生活态度，寄托了诗人对世俗世界的感慨与超脱之情。

《四季》："风水轮流转/和、熏、金、朔/都有风头出。"《忠告》："你成天让她呆在厨房/她怎能不让你/五味杂陈。"这两首诗中，"风头出""五味杂陈"，也是"旧词添新意"，颇耐品味。

## 意蕴浓厚的哲思美

"诗者，在心为志，发言为诗。""诗言志"是中国诗歌精神的密码，朱自清先生曾称之为中国诗歌的"开山的纲领"。好的诗歌，应当表达情怀、理想、志向，抒写人生洞见、精神火焰，展现出"诗性意义"。美学家雅克·马利坦在《艺术与诗中的创造性直觉》一书中说："诗性意义之于诗，恰如灵魂之于人。"一首诗只有情感而没有思想，就缺少了法国现代诗人瓦雷里所说的"理性的激动"，就会丧失持久的艺术震撼力。

正如诗人所说《诗》："一把测试/思维与情感深度与广度的/尺。"徐英才先生的三行诗，包含着对自然、社会、人生、理想、亲情、艺术等方涌的深刻思考，深沉浑厚、含蓄隽永。如《北风》："人间走一遭/无论如何也要/撼山，动地，卷狂澜。"这首诗展示了对自然界力量的赞美，更彰显了"潇洒走

"一回"的人生态度和撼动山川、搅动天地、掀起狂澜的勇气和决心。

又比如，《下海》："哪里有潮／哪里难免／此起彼伏。"诗人通过"潮"这一意象，隐喻了创业或人生道路上的波折与起伏。《海螺》："不净身／怎能／一人之下，万人之上。"暗示着只有经过"净身"这样极端的牺牲，才能换取极高的地位和权力，表达了一种对宫廷权力结构的讽刺或反思。《茶叶》："本不好争／一入湖，有了沉浮／就你推我搡。"诗人通过茶叶的"沉浮"与"你推我搡"的形态变化和相互碰撞，既展现了"人在江湖，身不由己"的残酷与无奈，也隐含了对人性复杂性的深刻洞察。

很显然，诗人对哲理的阐发不是"概念大于形象"的直白陈述，而是寓理于形象中，是运用生动的意象来含蓄表达的。

滴水藏瀚海，三行写大千。此刻，正是红红火火中国年。相信有更多像徐英才先生这样对微型诗的挚爱者，不断探索研究、实践创作、宣传推广微型诗，展示微型诗的无限魅力，微型诗这一"诗歌王国的微雕艺术"，一定能够更加红红火火，大放异彩。

幸得先生信任，妄而为序，诚惶诚恐。浅陋或不当之处，还请先生和读者诸君海涵。

寒山石

2025 年 1 月 31 日于古城西安

# Foreword

## The Poetic Beauty of the Three-Line World

### Xu Yingcai's
### *Gold Goblet Collection: 300 Three-Line Poems*

The beauty of poetry is boundless, encompassing the richness of thought, the authenticity of emotion, the refined taste of poetic essence, the elegance of language, the captivating allure of imagination, the lasting charm of artistic conception, the marvelous surprise of creativity, the perfection of rhythm, and the grace of form, among others. Writing poetry is a journey of exploration into the creation of beauty; reading poetry is a spiritual feast for the appreciation and enjoyment of poetic beauty. Reading *Gold Goblet Collection: 300 Three-Line Poems by Xu Yingcai* is like savoring a fine wine—each sip from the goblet intoxicates with its beauty.

### The Beauty of Concise Precision

Poetry is succinct, refined, and concise, yet never simplistic or crude. It values the highest degree of condensation and refinement, as Zhu Ziqing once said, "The more economical the language of poetry, the richer the emotions." Micro-poetry aims to express the richest and most captivating content with the most economical and concise language, transforming the limited into the infinite, capturing vastness in a tiny frame, and condensing thousands of miles into a small space.

Mr. Xu Yingcai's three-line poems excel in this art, using the fewest words to convey the richest content, the smallest space to express the deepest themes, and minimalism to evoke profound thoughts. This is just like what he expressed in his poem: "*My Poems* / Need not be as lengthy as the Yangtze River / Yet as deep and torrential / Filled with skies, high mountains, dense forests...” Therefore, when writing micro-poems, one must “Swing the sword within my heart's grasp / Sever glaciers, nudging them into the vast sea / Concealing the wellspring of life beneath the tip of the ice” (*Micro-Poems*). In the creation of his poetry, Mr. Xu seeks simplicity and conciseness. Some of his poems are as sharp and concise as a short sword or dagger, their poetic edge cutting straight to the heart."

For example, in *Di Flute,* with just four characters: "Ethereal / Sound / Drifts across the heavens," it vividly captures the lively image of both the transverse and vertical flutes, while perfectly conveying the enchanting beauty of heavenly music in a way that is utterly mesmerizing. In *Jiuzhaigou*: "Vale, vale / Each / Is a call," with just four characters and a clever use of homophony, the poet conveys a deep perception and unique expression of the breathtaking beauty of Jiuzhaigou.

*Misty Poetry*: "Dragon's / Claws / In clouds," uses only four brief characters. Through the metaphor "dragon's claws in clouds," it vividly presents an image that align with the poem's hazy, elusive qualities. The dragon's outstretched, powerful claws in the clouds symbolize the poem's deeper meaning—its critique of society, search for light, exploration of consciousness, and concern for humanity.

*Waves Washing the Sand:* "The history / Of / Figures" skillfully borrows the name of the classical Chinese poetry form *Wave Washing the Sand*. With just three characters, it vividly captures the themes that "all elegance will be swept away by wind and rain" and the idea that only through the great waves washing the sand can true gold be revealed.

These poems are not only linguistically concise but also rich in meaning, just as Zheng Banqiao once said, they have the charm of "accomplishing much with a little."

## The Unadorned Beauty of Simplicity

Poetry embodies both the grandeur and radiant beauty, as described in the phrase "majestic scenes and brilliant colors," and the simple, unadorned beauty, as found in the line "lotus blooms rising from clear water and naturally free from embellishment." The Ming Dynasty poet Qiu Jun, in his *Reply to a Friend on Poetry*, said: "The scenes before our eyes and the words on our lips are the most exquisite expressions of a poet." The famous Qing Dynasty essayist Yao Ding said, "There is no better artistic conception than simplicity; the choice of words and expression should seem as though they were naturally formed." The contemporary great poet Ai Qing also believed, "Profound and expansive thoughts, expressed through the simplest language, make the most ideal poetry."

Mr. Xu Yingcai's three-line poems capture his observations, thoughts, feelings, insights, and expressions, and can be described as "conveying the utmost flavor in simplicity." They are plain and concise, straightforward and easy to understand, with almost no obscure characters. Unadorned and unpretentious, they seem "naturally formed," yet every word and sentence strikes deeply at the heart, reaching the soul.

For example, in the poem *Flowers*: "Facing the sunlight / No matter how small / They shine with brilliance." This simple language inspires people to realize that as long as they face the sunlight with hope in their hearts, they can blossom with their own beauty and brilliance. *The Wind Chime*: "Brought from my hometown / Each sound / Clamors in my heart." In this simple narrative, the word "clamors" vividly conveys the deep, lingering feeling of homesickness, bringing it to life on the page.

Of course, "What seems ordinary is actually the most extraordinary; what appears easy is, in fact, the most difficult." The "simplicity" in "being simple" does not refer to the ordinary, but to the extraordinary within the ordinary. Similarly, the "lightness" in "being light" does not imply blandness, but rather richness within simplicity. The most dazzling eventually returns to simplicity; when the bustle of prosperity fades, true purity is revealed. Thus, the beauty of simplicity is the beauty born from refinement and perfection, the beauty that comes from returning to purity and truth. It is an artistic feature that arises only when the poet's artistic and intellectual cultivation mature together—one characterized by a subtle, inward energy and an outward simplicity.

For example, in *Who Has Hidden Away Spring*: "A few small birds / Probe with their claws / Everywhere in the snowy ground," the diction is simple yet tight, and the connection between words is both concise and seamless. The scene is created and described in a way that is natural yet full of imagination. *The Laughter Mother Brought Over*: "Steamy and lively / Echoes around the dinner table / Enveloping the entire family" is natural and smooth, seamless in its flow. It depicts a scene of happiness, warmth, and harmony. To quote Su Dongpo, the great Song poet, this "is not actually plain," but rather "extremely splendid."

## The Beauty of Vivid and Apt Imagery

"Words cannot fully convey the meaning, but the imagery can express it all." The Tang dynasty poetry critic Sikong Tu said, "When the imagery begins to emerge, nature has already worked its wonders." Imagery is both the fundamental component and functional unit of poetry. It is the soul and life of poetry, the very spirit of poetic art. Where there is imagery, there is poetry; where there is no imagery, there is no poetry.

"Mr. Xu Yingcai's use of imagery in his three-line poems is vivid and precise, displaying a uniquely ingenious touch."  For example, in *The Yangtze River Speaks*: "No one wields a sword sharper than mine —— / With a single surge, I cleave the land / Dividing south from north, warmth from cold, talents from generals," the imagery of the sharp "sword" metaphorically represents the Yangtze River, which splits the natural contrasts of warmth and cold between the north and south, as well as the cultural distinction of "southern scholars and northern generals." Through exaggeration, it vividly portrays the grandeur and might of the Yangtze River. *The Moon (II)*: "A rustic pouch/Brims with/The childhood tales Mother told me." In this poem, the "rustic pouch" serves as the central image, a vessel filled with deep emotions and cherished memories. It beautifully captures the greatness of a mother's love and the pure, innocent beauty of childhood moments.

For more examples, in *Spring Rain*: "A harp / Heavenly music emerges softly / The earth beams with joy." In *Autumn's Color*: "Strong yellow wine / One sip / Instant intoxication." In *Longing*: "Is a /Red bean sprout nestled in my heart / Drawing from my pulsing blood, growing day and night." In *Sunset (I)*: "A fiery red period /

Marking the end of another fruitful day / Leaping toward yet another brilliance." In *The Crescent Moon*: "A rhino horn / You on that side / And I, this."

The imagery of "harp," "yellow wine," "red bean branch," "period," and "rhino horn" in these poems are all very concrete, vivid, and lively. They serve multiple purposes—creating atmosphere, expressing emotions through the scenery, triggering associations, and conveying philosophical ideas. This significantly enhances the emotional impact of the poems. It can be said that the poet, with unique craftsmanship, skillfully handles these images, much like "a master of the craft, manipulating imagery with precision."

## The beauty of dynamic tension and bold leaps

The beauty of writing lies in its rise and fall. The Qing dynasty scholar Yuan Mei once said, "Writing is like viewing a mountain: flatness spoils the view." This means that writing should unfold with unexpected twists and turns, much like the peaks and valleys of a mountain, with monotony should be avoided at all costs. Similarly, poetry gains vitality, variation, and rich depth through its leaps and shifts.

Leaping (or "disjunction" as a technique term) is a fundamental aesthetic characteristic that distinguishes poetry from other literary forms. "Whether it's a leap in meaning, emotion, poetic focus, language, imagery, rhythm, or even time and space, all of these are essential means by which poetry gains elasticity, tension, subtlety, and ambiguity." They are also effective strategies for the ongoing creation and expansion of poetic space.

Just as the poet says in his *A Three-Line Poem*: "One line is the pot / The second is the plant / The third is the blue sky," which also showcases the beauty of disjunction. In his monograph *Chinese Three-Line Poetry: Theory and Techniques*, Mr. Xu Yingcai, from a creative perspective, introduces an internal structure known as the "three-step method" or "three-step progression," which mirrors the process of a long jump in athletics: the run-up (presenting the object), the take-off (embodying the object), and the leap (sublimating the object) ——ultimately reaching the farthest point of the poem. This is not only a leap in structure, but also a leap in meaning, as well as in the application of various techniques.

An example is *White Clouds*: "Fly, fly / Reach the West before night falls / Where you will be attired in the glowing Kaṣāya." In the leaps of imagery between the white clouds, the glowing, and the Kaṣāya (robe), the poem gains a sense of mystery and romanticism, endowing the white clouds with religious or sacred symbolism, and also showcasing the pursuit of freedom and beauty in life. Another example is *Father's Shoulder Pole*: "Time has pressed it / Into a heavy walking stick / My gaze often shifts from it to the house beam above." In the leaps of imagery between the shoulder pole, the walking stick, and the beam, the poem conveys the father's hard work and sacrifices, evoking the image of a "father's love as steadfast as a mountain" in the poet's heart.

Other examples include: *Empty Bench*: "The streetlight flickers on and off a few times / Yet the bench still awaits / Those intoxicating whispers." *Life*: "A mere speck of dust drifting westward / Unable to control itself, unaware of where or when it will land / So, why not float gracefully." *A River of Benevolence*: "I am a boat / Swift or slow my ride / I cannot depart from the river Mother excavated." A large number of such poems by the poet can be seen as the practical application of his 'three-step progression' theory in three-line poetry. These poems build strength and, in the final line, deliver a "last kick," completing the poetic sublimation and creating a breathtaking leap.

## The beauty of implicit, subtle and profound emotions

The method of expressing emotions in poetry encompasses both the bold and passionate, like a waterfall plunging downward, and the subtle and profound, like the deep, still waters longing to speak but remain silent. The implicit beauty is a universal artistic pursuit in classical Chinese poetry, emphasizing the principles of "words near, but emotions distant," "meaning near, but intent far," "implied, not overt," with a lingering aftertaste. "Liu Xie, in *The Literary Mind and the Carving of Dragons,* says: "Deep literature is veiled in elegance, with a lingering aftertaste wrapped in subtlety." This means that when an article is written with depth, it carries an inherent beauty, concealing flavors that lie beyond the surface.

Mr. Xu Yingcai's three-line poetry, especially his lyrical poems, does not feature the passionate, unrestrained outpouring of emotions, but instead is subtle and implicit, with simple language yet deep feelings, carrying profound meaning. In what seems like an ordinary narrative, the poet's intense emotions are concealed.

For example, in *Spring Melody*: "Morning sky, a blank sheet of paper; the power cables, guiding lines / Above, a flock of birds arranges its notes /—— Down, hundreds of mud-caked performers spill out from the village." The poet, through creative metaphors, paints a vivid picture of a rural spring morning brimming with life and vitality, expressing admiration for the laborers. *A Path in My Hometown*: "Winding and winding / Each bend cradles my longing / Each curve tugs at my heart and soul." At first glance, it may seem like gentle ripples, yet with simple language, clear imagery, and heartfelt expression, it successfully tugs at the reader's heartstrings. *Not a Legend*: "Never seen an iron bar ground into a needle / But seen mother flatten our washboard / Through dozens of sweltering summers and frigid winters." This poem, too, is emotionally restrained and profound, stirring a strong, heartfelt response.

The poet's three-line poems about his father embody an even deeper beauty—restrained, enduring, and subtly profound. For example: *Father (II)*: "A masterpiece of Nature / His wrinkled brow, sculpted by the wind / Bronzed skin, painted by the sun." *The Past (I)*: "All etched in relief / On father's callused palms / Hard to erase." This creates a vivid image of a hardworking and touching figure through the expressive depiction of the father's wrinkles, skin, and calluses. *Father (III)*: "Single-minded / Tends the fields alone, yet keeps me from his toil / Insisting I plow the world of words." *The Road*: "Father has walked / Roughly etched upon his brow / He doesn't want to pass it down to us." *The Spinning Top (II)*: "Father never stops whipping / Each whip / Is love." Thus, in what seems like a calm narrative, it reveals the deep and great love of a father, as well as the infinite hope of all fathers who wish for their children to succeed.

Of course, the art of concealing without revealing and hiding without exposing lies in hiding what should be hidden, concealing what should be concealed, exposing what should be exposed, and showing what should be shown. This is a wisdom of choice. "Focusing solely on concealment or hiding makes the work obscure and hard to grasp; focusing only on revealing or showing drains it of its poetic essence." Concealment is for the sake of better revelation, and hiding is for the sake of better expression. The key is to have depth—the poetic flavor, emotional resonance, thematic meaning, and engaging charm—that invites thoughtful reflection and creates space to inspire and ignite the reader's imagination. The poet must be deeply attuned to this craft. Therefore, when we read the poet's three-line poems, we are able to pull out the hidden, profound emotions from the emotional threads the poet reveals or expresses.

## The visual beauty of what words depict

"The visual beauty of what words depict" comes from Liu Xie's *The Literary Mind and the Carving of Dragons • The Color of Objects,* where he describes how precise and vivid language allows one to "see" the shape of a scene. This echoes the ancient saying, "It is difficult to describe a scene as if it were right before your eyes." This is universally true. Whether in China or the West, there is the notion "poetry and painting share the same origin." Zhang Shunmin of the Northern Song dynasty further believed in his *Postscript to the Poetry and Paintings of Bai Zhi* that "Poetry is a formless painting, and painting is a form of poetry." The ancient Greek poet Simonides also proposed, "Poetry is a painted sound, just as painting is a silent poem." The French classical critic Racin said, "The conception in poetry is like the composition of a painting."

Mr. Xu Yingcai's three-line poems, with just a few strokes, often bring us the visual beauty of what words depict. His poetry can truly be said to embody "painting within poetry," vivid and lifelike.

For example, in *Receding Twilight*: "At the end of the road / The old man's elongated shadow slowly fades / On the horizon, the deep evening glow gradually wanes." This is a portrait of old age, of life's inevitable twilight. Through the delicate depiction of the old man's shadow and the fading twilight, it conveys the theme of time passing and the aging of life. The poem is filled with the lingering charm of years gone by and a quiet sorrow, while also urging to cherish the present and seize every fleeting moment in life.

*Spring Thunder*: "Wakes the dreaming butterfly / She peeks out of her cocoon hut, looking around / For the path to tour spring." This is a picture of all things in nature awakening in anticipation of spring. Through the imagery of spring thunder rousing the butterflies, and employing personification, it vividly portrays the arrival of spring and the revival of nature, while also expressing people's love for and longing for the season."

*Night Sky (II)*: "A lonely goose / Crosses the full moon / Yearning to restore the broken mirror." This is a picture of a solitary goose eclipsing the full moon. Through the imagery of the lone goose, the full moon, and the broken mirror, the poem conveys the poet's profound reflection on the inevitable separations and solitude in life, while also expressing a yearning for reunion and completeness.

*The Plow*: "Father's back— / Which soil flower / Doesn't bloom with his back arched?" *An Old Farmer*: "With a hoe in hand / He pulls the sun from east to west / Then shoulders the crescent moon downhill." It vividly displays the poet's admiration for his father and the old farmers, as well as the poet's deep and intense emotions.

Wings: "Left hand holding Dad / Right hand holding Mom / I am a bird that flies." This is a tender and sweet portrayal of three people. It effectively expresses the deep emotional bond between the child and the parents, as well as the child's longing for the freedom to soar. Not only does it convey the warmth of family and the strength of kinship, but it also sparks boundless imagination about freedom, exploration, and growth. More importantly, it highlights the vital role a complete family plays in a child's development. Only in a complete family can a child spread their wings and soar; in a broken family, the child lacks the wings to fly freely.

# The astonishing beauty of unceasing inventive ideas

Astonishment is one of the most essential characteristics of poetry, the source of poetic vitality, and an important manifestation of the poet's creativity. This astonishing beauty is manifested in many aspects, such as: the striking originality in exploring ideas, the ability to "say what has never been said before," the clever, marvelous, and fresh use of language with its techniques of "defamiliarization," "abnormalization," or "peculiarization," the unique and unconventional perspectives, and various other expressive forms, all of which offer a refreshing experience for the reader.

Mr. Xu Yingcai's three-line poems often find the extraordinary in the ordinary, opening up new and unique perspectives. For example, *Waves*: "The Longing / of / Waters" composed of just four words is it's almost a stroke of genius. It captures the river's characteristic yearning to continually surge into great waves, symbolizing the lofty aspirations of those with ambition. It also reflects the poet's inner emotions and his reverence and admiration for nature."

In *Erhu Solo "Water of Sorrow"*: "One string is the left bank, the other the right bank / Roars in between / The cry of a nation's struggle for strength," The poet's use of two strings to metaphorically represent "the left bank" and "the right bank" is indeed a stroke of brilliant imagination. Meanwhile, the phrase "Roars in between / The cry of a nation's struggle for strength" evokes the deep sorrow and unyielding spirit of resistance that the nation has endured, telling the story of its unceasing self-improvement and the journey of struggle.

*The Fleeting Flower*: "Opening its bright floral eyes / It sees a world full of dust / And closes them that very day." This poem brings a fresh perspective to the fleeting beauty of the epiphyllum, not only praising its beauty and nobility but also using it as a metaphor for a life attitude that is detached, beyond worldly concerns. It reflects the poet's feelings of both longing and transcendence, finding solace beyond the mundane.

*Four Seasons*: "The tide turns / Gentle breeze, warm breeze, autumn wind, and north wind / Each has its time to shine" and *Sincere Advice*: "You make her stay in the kitchen all the time / How could she not become / A blend of every flavor to you?" In these two poems, phrases like "time to shine " and "a blend of every flavor" demonstrate the technique of "old words with new meaning," which are quite thought-provoking and worth savoring.

## The profound beauty of philosophical contemplation

"Poetry is born from the heart as intent, and expressed through words as poetry." "Poetry as intent" is the key to the spirit of Chinese poetry. Mr. Zhu Ziqing once called it the "foundational principle" of Chinese poetry. Good poetry should convey emotions, ideals, and aspirations, articulate insights into life and the flames of the spirit, and reveal the inherent "poetic meaning." The aesthete Jacques Maritain, in his book *Creative Intuition in Art and Poetry*, said: "The poetic meaning in poetry is like the soul in a person." A poem that possesses only emotion but lacks thought misses what the French modern poet Valéry referred to as the "excitement of reason," and thus loses its lasting artistic impact.

As the poet himself puts it in *Poetry*: "A measure / of the depth and breadth / of thought and emotion." Mr. Xu Yingcai's three-line poems contain profound reflections on nature, society, life, ideals, family, art, and more. They are deep, rich, subtle, and enduring. For example, *The North Wind*: "Venturing into the mortal world / No matter what / I'll shake mountains, stir the earth, and churn raging waves." This poem displays admiration for the power of nature, while also highlighting the life attitude of living bold and carefree life, embodying the courage and determination to shake mountains, stir the earth, and set off wild waves.

Another example is *Venturing into the Sea*: "Where tides exist / There the inevitability of / Rising and falling." The poet uses the image of "tides" as a metaphor for the ups and downs one encounters on the path of entrepreneurship or in life itself, suggesting the inescapable fluctuations and challenges that come with it. *A Conch*: "Without purification / How can it be / Below one, yet above ten thousand?" This suggests that only through extreme sacrifices, such as "castration," can one attain high status and power, expressing a satire or reflection on the power structure within the court. *Tea Leaves*: "Not inherently meant to compete / But once in the lake, there's rise and fall / Then comes the pushing and shoving." Through the "rising and sinking" of the tea leaves and their "pushing and shoving" as they change form and collide, the poet not only illustrates the cruel and helpless reality of "one cannot control their fate in the world," but also a deep insight into the complexity of human nature.

Clearly, the poet's philosophical expression is not a blunt statement where "concepts outweigh images," but rather a technique where meaning is conveyed through imagery. The poet uses vivid images to subtly communicate deeper ideas.

A drop of water holds the vast ocean, and three lines can encapsulate the grand world. At this very moment, it is the vibrant and flourishing Chinese New Year. I believe that more enthusiasts, like Mr. Xu Yingcai, who are passionate about micro-poetry, will continue to explore, research, create, and promote it, unveiling its boundless charm. As the "micro-sculpture art" of the poetic world, micro-poetry is sure to thrive and shine even brighter.

By Mr. Xu's trust, I humbly write this preface, filled with both gratitude and trepidation. Should there be any shortcomings or inadequacies, I kindly ask for the patience and understanding of Mr. Xu and the esteemed readers."

Written by: Han Shan Shi
January 31, 2025, in the ancient city of Xi'an

# 目　录
# Table of Contents

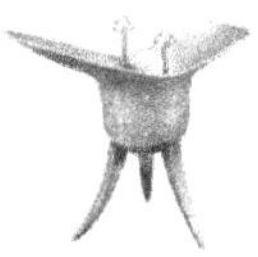

# ~1~

# 白云

飞吧，飞吧
入夜前赶到西天
能穿上霞光焰焰的袈裟

## White Clouds

*Fly, fly*
*Reach the West before night falls*
*Where you will be attired in the glowing Kaṣāya**

Note: *Kaṣāy is a Buddhist robe.*

# ~2~

# 北风

人间走一遭
无论如何也要
撼山，动地，卷狂澜


## The North Wind


*Venturing into the mortal world*
*No matter what*
*I'll shake mountains, stir the earth, and churn raging waves*

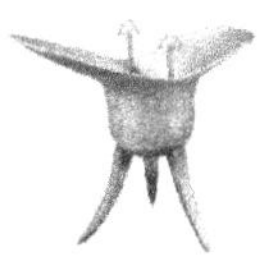

# ~3~

## 并非传说

没见过铁棒磨成针
见过母亲用数十个寒暑
磨平了衣板上的木棱

### Not a Legend

*Never seen an iron bar ground into a needle**
*But seen mother flatten our washboard*
*Through dozens of sweltering summers and frigid winters*

*Note: Legend has it that young Li Bai, one of the greatest poets of the Tang Dynasty, witnessed an old woman grinding an iron bar into a needle, an act that inspired his later diligence.*

~*4*~

草

小得微不足道
可是，没有它们
—— 还有春天吗？

**Grasses**

*Tiny and unnoticeable*
*But without them*
*—— Could there still be spring?*

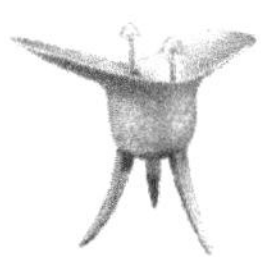

# ~5~

# 草茵

身上为什么
鸟儿蹦跳，儿童欢跑，情侣偎依……
难道不是因为它生性温和还接地气

## *The Meadow*

*Why upon its body*
*Do birds hop, children frolic, lovers cuddle…*
*Is it not because of its gentle nature and grounding presence?*

# ~6~

## 茶叶

本不好争
一入湖，有了沉浮
就你推我搡

*Tea Leaves*

*Not inherently meant to compete*
*But once in the lake*, there's rise and fall*
*Then comes the pushing and shoving*

*Note: The word "lake" is the English translation of 湖 (hú), which is homophonic to 壶 (hú, meaning "pot"). The expression 江湖 (jiāng hú), meaning "lakes and rivers," refers to society in Chinese.*

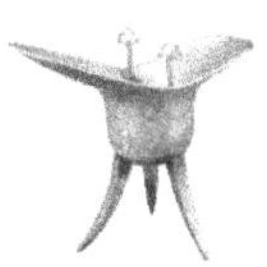

# ~7~

# 蝉（一）

面壁参天大树
修到脱胎换骨
方遁入空中

## *Cicada (I)*

*Facing the towering tree in solitude*
*It meditates until it sheds its old form*
*Only then does it ascend into the vast sky*

# ~*8*~

# 蝉（二）

未经黑暗的煎熬
脱胎换壳的磨砺
怎能引歌高亢

## *Cicada (II)*

*Without the torment of darkness*
*And the trials of shedding its form*
*How can its song resonate triumphantly*

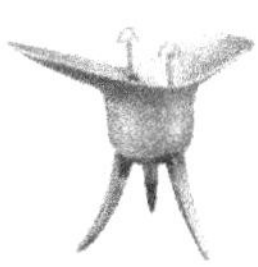

# ~9~

## 蝉语

声声　直刺燥热的尘世
几人听懂其禅意：
执了——、执了——

### The Cicada's Chirping

*Sound by sound, it pierces the sweltering, dust-choked world*
*How many truly understand its Zen meaning:*
*Zhi-liao, zhi-liao**

*Note:* "Zhi-liao" comes from the Chinese phrase 执了 *(zhí liǎo, meaning 'attached'),* which is homophonic to 知了 *(zhí liǎo)* the Chinese common name for cicada and also the sound this insect makes.

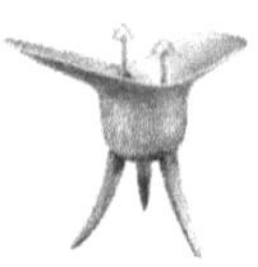

# ~10~

# 长江说

谁的剑也没我的犀利
一洪劈开
南北　温寒　还有才与将

## *The Yangtze River Speaks*

*No one wields a sword sharper than mine ——*
*With a single surge, I cleave the land*
*Dividing south from north, warmth from cold, talents from generals**

*Note: Southern China is much warmer than Northern China. While the former is said to have more talented people, the latter produces more generals.*

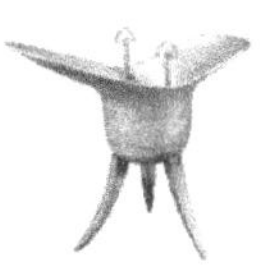

# ~11~

# 晨景

雾
掩住了天桥、高架、大厦
掩不住霓虹闪烁、车灯川流……

## *A Morning Scene*

*Fog*
*Veils the skybridges, overpasses, and towers*
*Yet cannot obscure the flickering neon, the ceaseless streams of*
*headlights…*

# ~12~

# 翅膀

左手拉着爸
右手拉着妈
我是一只会飞的鸟

## Wings

*Left hand holding Dad*
*Right hand holding Mom*
*I am a bird that flies*

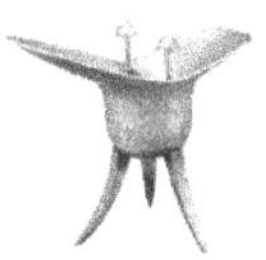

# ~*13*~

## 尺子

揪着你就论长道短
长了，就砍你的头，剁你的脚
短了，就弃你在阴暗的角落

## *Tape Measure*

*Grabbing you, it measures your length and width ——*
*If you're too long, it will sever your head, or lop off your feet*
*If you're too short, it will abandon you into a shadowed corner*

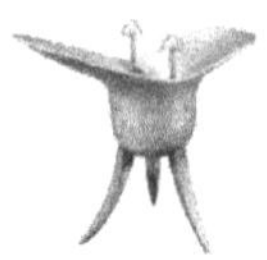

## ~14~

# 垂暮

路的尽头
老人拖长的身影慢慢淡去
天边　那抹浓厚的晚霞也渐渐消隐

### *Receding Twilight*

*At the end of the road*
*The old man's elongated shadow slowly fades*
*On the horizon, the deep evening glow gradually wanes*

# ~*15*~

## 锤子

抓住你就猛揍一顿
直到你缩下头沉下腰
卡在两重天动弹不得

### *Hammer*

*Grab hold of you and strike hard*
*Until you shrink your head and sink your shoulder*
*Trapped between two heavens, unable to move*

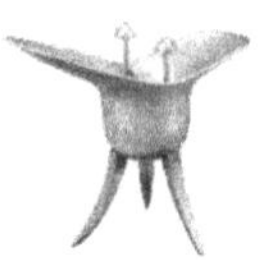

# ~16~

# 春风（一）

定然手执无形的彩绘喷笔
要不，它所到之处
为何都洇出了姹紫嫣红


## Spring Breeze (I)

*It must hold an invisible, colorful spray pen*
*For wherever it goes*
*Why do vibrant hues of purples and reds bloom?*

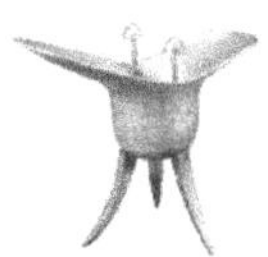

# ~*17*~

# 春风（二）

执一支彩笔
这里涂涂，那里抹抹
便勾去了我的心魂

## Spring Breeze (II)

*With a brush in hand*
*It paints here and there*
*And sweeps away my heart and soul*

# ~*18*~

# 春光

都说难留
我心里为何总有
诧紫嫣红

## **Springtime**

*Is said to be fleeting*
*Yet why in my heart always resides*
*A riot of colors*

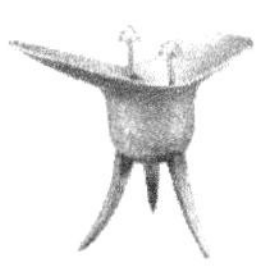

# ~19~

# 春景

柳　倾身戏水
溪　含情仰望
燕　在其中传情

## Spring Scene

*The willow leans over, playfully stroking the water*
*The stream rises up, affectionately looking on*
*A swallow flits between them, conveying messages of love*

# ~20~

# 春雷

惊醒了梦睡的蝶
她探头蛹屋外，四下张望
踏春的路


## Spring Thunder

*Wakes the dreaming butterfly*
*She peeks out of her cocoon hut, looking around*
*For the path to tour spring*

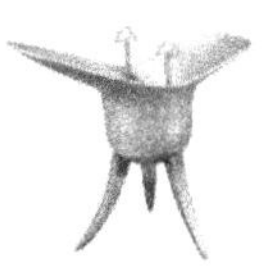

# ~*21*~

## 春曲

晨空当纸　电缆作线
上面，一大群小鸟在摆谱
下面，村口涌出数百泥脚演奏者

### ***Spring Melody***

*Morning sky, a blank sheet of paper; the power cables, guiding lines*
*Above, a flock of birds arranges its notes*
*Down, hundreds of mud-caked performers spill out from the village*

# ~22~

# 春序

冰冷的雪
火样的梅
真情终将溶化无情


**Prelude to Spring**

*Cold snow*
*Fire-like plum blossoms*
*True feelings will eventually melt the cold indifference*

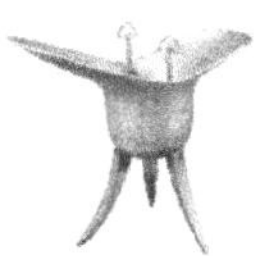

# ~23~

# 春雨

竖琴
天籁轻起
大地喜形于色

## Spring Rain

*A harp*
*Heavenly music emerges softly*
*The earth beams with joy*

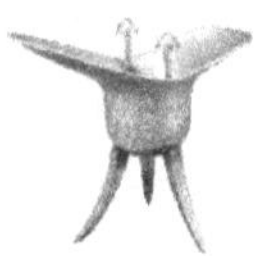

# ~24~

# 大红袍

红得发紫
下海后
都褪了色

## ***Da Hong Pao****

*So red it almost turns purple*
*Once in the sea**
*It fades*

*Note: 1. Da Hong Pao is a transliteration of the tea name* 大红袍 *(dà hóng páo, Big Red Robe Tea).*

*2. "In the sea" is the translation of the Chinese phrase* 下海 *(xià hǎi). While* 下海 *literally means "to enter the sea," it figuratively means "to get involved in business."*

# ~25~

## 大海

躺在红霞燃烧的西天下
哼那远古洪荒的
歌

### The Vast Sea

*Lying beneath the burning red glow of the western sky*
*It hums the ancient, eternal*
*Ballad of the primordial world*

# ~26~

大风里

重
者
坚守底线

## *In Big Wind*

*What is*
*Heavy*
*Sticks to the bottom line*

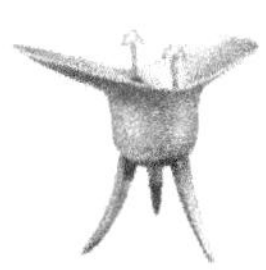

# ~*27*~

## 殚精竭虑

怀念
试图挣脱思之壳
却被一次次无情弹回

### *Strained Thoughts*

*Longing*
*Struggles to break free from the cocoon of thoughts*
*But relentlessly bounced back, again and again*

# ~28~

稻草

出身泥乡
编织起来
度过多少人到达远方

**The Straws**

*Born in the muddy countryside*
*Once woven up*
*It has taken many to distant lands*

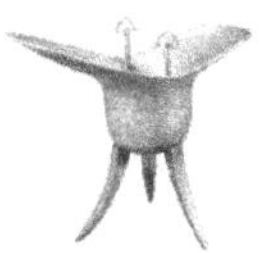

# ~29~

## 稻草人

生来本该让鸟啄食
如今背靠蓝天　手执蒲扇
就耀武扬威起来

### *Scarecrow*

*Born to be pecked by birds*
*Now, with the sky behind it and a fan in hand*
*It stands, proud and imposing*

# ~30~

## 等待

她在站台上
焦急地等待
车把她送到心轨交汇的远方


### *Waiting*

*On the platform*
*She waits anxiously for the train to take her*
*To where her heart and rails converge in the distant place*

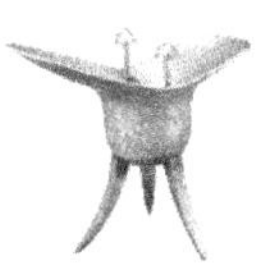

# ~31~

# 等雪

你出行那天下雪
明知你回家时不一定有雪
我仍心焦地等着另一场雪

## Waiting for Snowfall

*You left on a snowy day*
*I know you may not return to snowy weather*
*Yet, I still wait anxiously for another snowfall*

# ~32~

# 灯火

十年
把投在陋室泥地上的影子
送进了高等学府

## The Lamp Light

*For ten years*
*It has sent the shadow on the humble room's muddy ground*
*Into a prestigious institution*

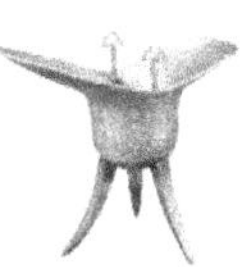

# ~33~

笛

妙
音
横空

## *Di Flute**

*Ethereal*
*Sound*
*Drifts across the heavens*

*Note: The di flute is a Chinese musical instrument played horizontally.*

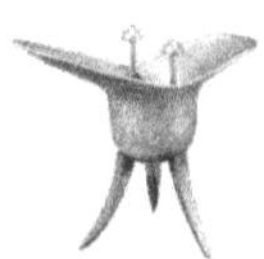

# ~34~

# 订书针

小得无足轻重
但毕生聚拢的
都不无价值

## A Staple

*Small and insignificant*
*Yet everything it binds*
*Is not without worth*

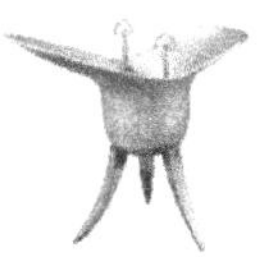

# ~35~

# 钓鱼

不倒松下
一老者手执鱼竿
鱼钩　在倒映的风云里静候

## *Fishing*

*Beneath a pine that never falls*
*An elder grips his fishing rod with care*
*Its hook, quietly awaits in the inverted wind and clouds*

# ~36~

## 丢失的日子

翻看日历
2020 处
一个虫蛀的大窟窿

### The Lost Days

*Flipping through the calendar*
*I reach the year 2020 ——*
*Where there's a worm-eaten hole*

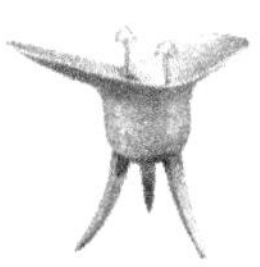

# ~37~

冬

用寒流　朔风　漫雪
把苍翠嫣红的春
挤进期盼的心角


## *Winter*

*With cold currents, northern winds, and drifting snow,*
*It squeezes the verdant greens and crimson reds of spring*
*Into the corner of an eager heart*

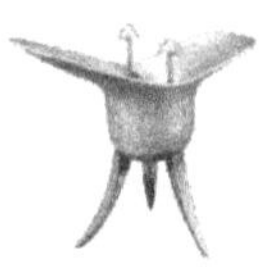

# ~38~

# 都市的夜

像暗房里横晾的胶片
那一扇扇亮着灯的窗
是曝着光的生活原型

## A Metropolitan Night

*Like film hanging in a darkroom*
*Those windows, each alight*
*Are prototypes of life exposed to the world*

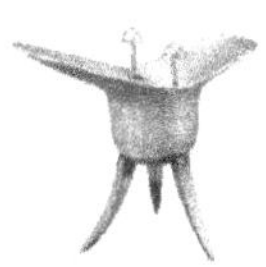

# ~39~

## 断裂的春

被炮弹震落的满地樱花泪瓣
被弹片削剩的半截农舍的身子
在残阳里述说……

### The Broken Spring

*Cherry blossom petal tears, shattered and scattered by bombs*
*And the half-destroyed body of a farmhouse, carved away by*
*shrapnel*
*Tell the tale in the setting sun...*

# ~40~

# 二胡

俩
才能
互述衷肠　妮妮动人

## Two-Stringed Fiddle

*Two*
*Can exchange*
*Heartfelt feelings, captivating and poignant*

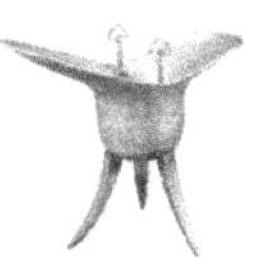

# ~*41*~

二胡独奏（一）

弦上
分明奔腾着
千军万马

**Erhu Solo (I)**

*On the strings*
*Clearly gallop*
*Myriad horses and soldiers*

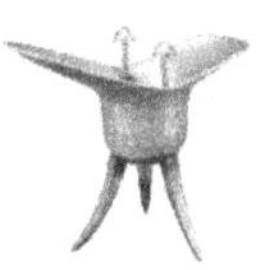

# ~42~

# 二胡独奏（二）

要去草原亲领天高地阔
不如在两根弦上
心领万马奔腾

## *Erhu Solo (II)*

*To go to the prairie, to witness the vast sky and land*
*Is not as authentic as letting your heart ride*
*A thousand horses galloping on two strings*

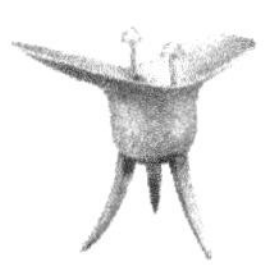

# ~43~

## 二胡独奏《江河水》

一根弦是左岸　一根弦是右岸
中间咆哮的
是民族自强的呐喊

### *Erhu Solo "Water of Sorrow"*

*One string is the left bank, the other the right bank*
*Roars in between*
*The cry of a nation's struggle for strength*

# ~44~

二泉印月

为何
双膝跪地才能听懂
难道需要接上地气

## The Moon's Reflection in the Spring

*Why only by kneeling down*
*Can one fathom the music*
*Does it require grounding*

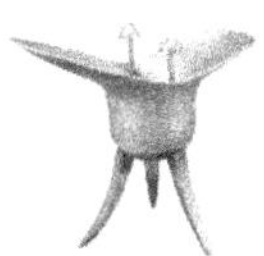

# ~45~

# 帆

无论多轻微
放开束缚，顶住风浪
就能远行

## *Sail*

*No matter how light*
*If you can shed your constraints and withstand wind and waves*
*You can journey far*

# ~46~

# 帆船

风浪里的
海
鸥

## *Sailboat*

*A seagull on wind
And
Waves*

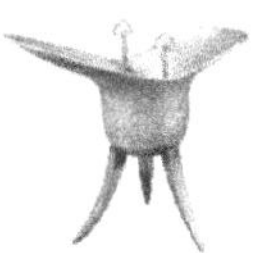

## ~47~

# 风

挥动无形长鞭
催云　驱浪　勃万物
画一幅悠悠天地动态图


**Wind**

*Wielding an unseen, long whip*
*It drives the clouds, stirs the waves, invigorates all things*
*A vast, dynamic canvas of heaven and earth in motion*

# ~48~

# 风铃

老家带来的
每一声
都闹在心上

## The Wind Chime

*Brought from my hometown*
*Each sound*
*Clamors in my heart*

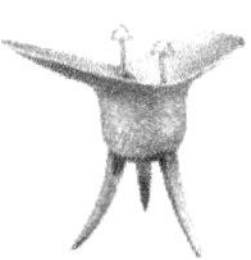

# ~49~

风景

是啊，风景、风景
没一窝风
哪来景

## Scenery

*Yes, scenery, scenery* ——*
*Without a whirl of wind*
*Where is the scene?*

Note: The Chinese for "scenery" is 风景 (fēng jǐng), which means "wind" and "scene."

# ~50~

# 风铃

风真地来了
爱叽喳的山雀躲了起来
沉默的它　却唱起了歌

## **Wind Chimes**

*When the wind actually comes*
*The chatter-loving sparrows hide away*
*Yet, the quiet bell begins to sing*

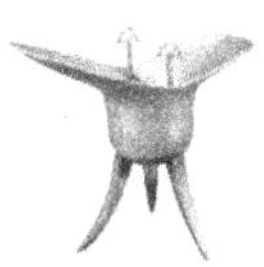

# ~51~

## 枫树

万物凋敝时
是它们用周身的气血
焕发出最后一道亮丽风景

### Maple Trees

*When all else withers*
*They give all their blood*
*To unfold one last, glorious display*

# ~52~

# 父亲（一）

每当看到那弓起的山脊
就想到你的背
我不清楚这印象来自你的重压还是伟岸

## *Father (I)*

*Every time I see that rising mountain ridge*
*I think of your back ——*
*Not sure if this impression comes from your heavy burden or*
*towering strength*

# ~53~

# 父亲（二）

大自然的杰作
额上的皱纹　由风雕成
浑身的古铜色　太阳漆出

## *Father (II)*

*A masterpiece of Nature*
*His wrinkled brow, sculpted by the wind*
*Bronzed skin, painted by the sun*

# ~54~

# 父亲（三）

一根筋
自己种地，却不让我下田
要我在文字里耕耘

## Father (III)

*Single-minded*
*Tends the fields alone, yet keeps me from his toil*
*Insisting I plow the world of words*

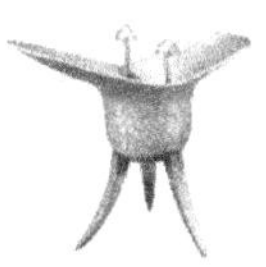

# ~55~

## 父亲的扁担

已被岁月压成
沉重的拐棍
我的眼光常从它移向那根屋梁


### Father's Shoulder Pole

*Time has pressed it*
*Into a heavy walking stick*
*My gaze often shifts from it to the house beam above*

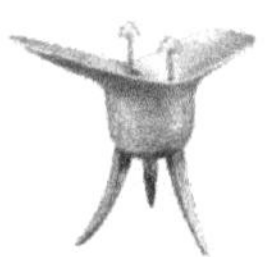

# ~56~

# 钢琴

黑白两道
联欢时
便是快乐和谐的交响日

## *Piano*

*When black and white*
*Unite grandly*
*Joy and harmony resonate in symphony*

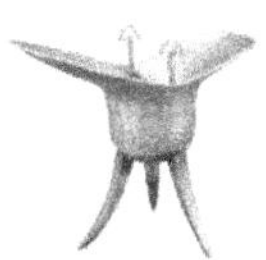

# ~57~

# 根（一）

在黑暗中下探
挺起胸膛 迎接太阳的
途径

## *Roots (I)*

*Reaching deep into darkness*
*To seek a path to rise*
*And stand tall, chest open to the sun*

# 根（二）

没它蜷缩在黑暗里
日夜操持
它头上怎会满目苍翠

## ***Roots (II)***

*Without huddling in the dark*
*Toiling day and night*
*How could they lift their heads to the lush green overhead*

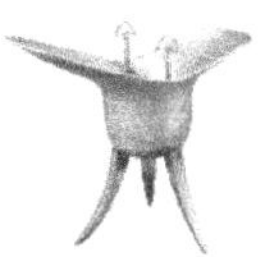

# ~59~

# 空椅子

路灯几度点亮
它仍在等待
那些醉人的蜜语

## Empty Bench

*The streetlight flickers on and off a few times*
*Yet the bench still awaits*
*Those intoxicating whispers*

# ~60~

# 鼓（一）

压力越大
震动越大
响声越大

## The Drum (I)

*The greater the pressure*
*The greater the vibration*
*The louder the sound*

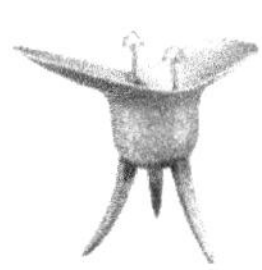

# ~61~

# 鼓（二）

咚咚咚，震撼声
来自紧绷与压力
绷得越紧压力越大，声音越响

## Drum (II)

*Boom boom boom, the resounding sound*
*Comes from tension and pressure*
*The tighter the strain, the greater the pressure, the louder the boom*

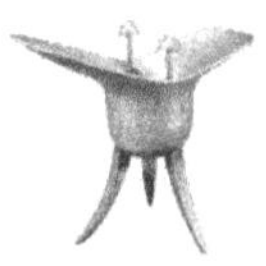

# ~62~

## 孤独的月牙

拽着白云的衣角不舍
无情的风来了
抓起云的衣袂就走

### The Lonely Crescent

*Clutching the hem of a white cloud, unwilling to let go*
*The heartless wind arrives*
*Seizes the cloud's garment and carries her away*

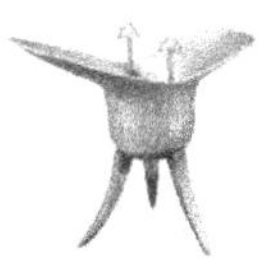

# ~63~

## 骨骼

貌似嶙峋无魂
却承载了
灵与肉　智与情

### *Skeleton*

*Though appearing jagged and devoid of soul*
*It bears*
*Spirit and flesh, mind and heart*

# ~64~

# 故乡

你没有让我骨瘦形消
因你每晚都步行千里
来窗前伴我入眠

## Hometown

*You did not let me pine*
*For every night, you walk a thousand miles*
*To my window, to keep me company as I sleep*

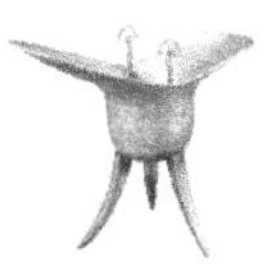

# ~65~

## 故乡的小路

弯弯曲曲
每一弯　都挽着我的怀念
每一曲　都勾着我的心魂

### *A Path in My Hometown*

*Winding and winding*
*Each bend cradles my longing*
*Each curve tugs at my heart and soul*

# ~66~

# 古筝独奏

心音
在云朵
漂游

## *Zither Solo*

*Heart's melody*
*Wandering*
*In the clouds*

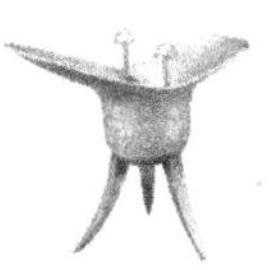

# ~67~

## 馆藏图书

一排排微微倾身站立
准备起跑　　引领
坐着的腾飞


### Library Collection

*Rows upon rows, they stand slightly leaning*
*Ready to race, leading*
*the seated to soar*

# ~68~

## 寒秋

又遭连夜雨
遍地黄叶
数声雁鸣勾我心魂同行

### *Cold Autumn*

*Once again, a night of relentless rain*
*Yellow leaves scattered all around*
*A few honks of geese took my heart to journey with them*

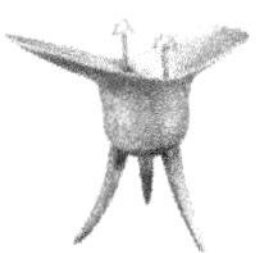

# ~*69*~

## 光

哪怕一路荆棘
也永远大步直直地走
从不退却

### **Light**

*Even on a path of thorns*
*It strides forward, unwavering*
*Never retreating*

# ~*70*~

## 海螺

不净身
怎能
一人之下，万人之上

### *A Conch*

*Without purification*
*How can it be*
*Below one, yet above ten thousand?*

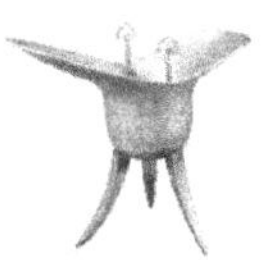

## ~71~

# 荷花（一）

本有蜻蜓沾惹　浮萍缠绕
为何总还在月下轻舞
锲而不舍地等待

## Lotus Flower (I)

*Dragonflies tease you, duckweed flirts with you ——*
*Why do you keep dancing beneath the moon*
*Steadfastly waiting, never giving in*

# ~72~

# 荷花（二）

玉立污泥
不为蜻蜓轻叩心门，不为皎月托思乡愁
是以身示尘：寒地也出贵人


## *Lotus Flower (II)*

*Standing like jade in the mud*
*Not for dragonflies to touch her heart, nor for the moon to cradle homesick longings*
*But to show the world: even from humble soil, the noble emerges*

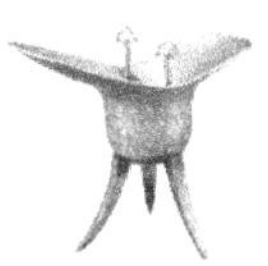

## ~73~

# 荷的心思

被蜻蜓点开
不然　她为何侧过风
害羞地左避右躲却又并不闪开

### *The Lotus' Heart*

*Touched open by a dragonfly*
*Otherwise, why would she turn from the wind*
*Shyly swaying, yet never fully retreating*

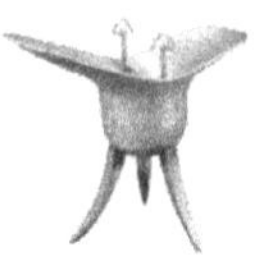

# ~74~

## 红尘

一只沙漏
里面熙熙攘攘你推我搡
其实哪个不是走向漏口

### The Mundane World

*An hourglass:*
*Inside, a bustling crowd jostles and shuffles*
*But which grain isn't heading toward the narrowing end?*

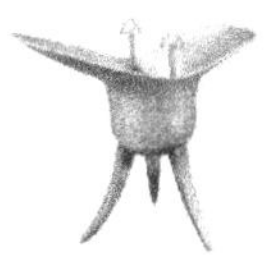

# ~75~

## 蝴蝶

生来并无翅膀，也无牙齿
硬是用它的唾液
融化出一条通天的路

### *Butterfly*

*Born without wings, nor teeth*
*Yet with mere saliva*
*It melts open a path to the heavens*

# ~76~

## 蝴蝶馆

本可在蓝天谱写篇章
却在五间七间蝶房里
自命不凡

### *The Butterfly House*

*They could script their chapters in the azure sky*
*Yet, they glorify themselves*
*Confined within five or seven exhibition rooms*

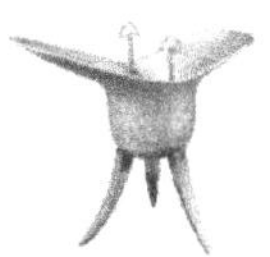

# ~77~

## 蝴蝶的心形翅翼

是上帝特意打造
还是无意的巧合
——看它们在蓝天成双成对地追逐

## **Heart-Shaped Wings of Butterflies**

*Are they deliberately crafted by God
Or a fortunate coincidence?
—— Look at them chasing each other in pairs in the blue sky*

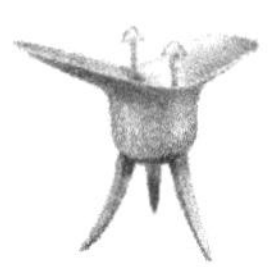

# ~78~

# 画眉与老鹰

老鹰嗓音刺耳，却闻名遐迩
画眉嗓音甜美，却小为人知
——擅飞不擅飞而已


## Thrush and Eagle

*The eagle's call is harsh, yet known far and wide*
*The thrush's song is sweet, yet remains obscure*
*—— It's all about flying skills*

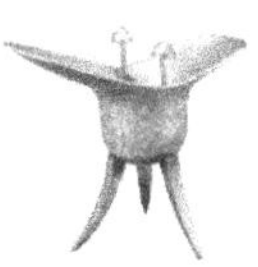



# 花

面朝阳光
再小
也灿烂

## *Flowers*

*Facing the sunlight*
*No matter how small*
*They shine with brilliance*

# ~*80*~

# 花瓶

把一块泥
捏成舞姿，纹上美图
空心也吸引眼球


## *Vase*

*Shape a lump of clay*
*Into a dancing pose and etch it with beautiful patterns*
*Even the hollow captivates the eye*

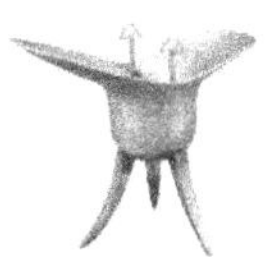

# ~81~

## 花的世界

无数雨花簇拥着
一朵油纸伞花　花下拢着
一对盛开的心花

### The World in Bloom

*Countless raindrops in bloom clustering*
*An umbrella in bloom, beneath which*
*a pair of hearts in bloom*

# ~82~

# 划船

满湖的星
最令我神往的
是船上朝着我忽闪的那对

## ***Rowing***

*Amidst the stars filling the lake*
*What enchants me most*
*Is the pair on the boat, twinkling at me*

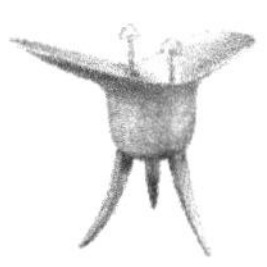

# ~83~

# 黄河（一）

跌宕咆哮
曲尽五千年
自强史

## Yellow River (I)

*Surging and roaring*
*Through the twists and turns of five thousand years*
*A history of self-strengthening*

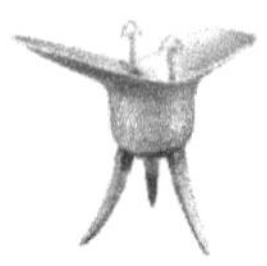

# ~84~

# 黄河（二）

蜿蜒　奔腾　金灿灿
它到底是条江还是龙
地质学家这样说　历史学家那样说

## The Yellow River (II)

*Winding, roaring, shimmering in golden rays*
*Is it a river or a dragon?*
*Geologists say this, historians say that*

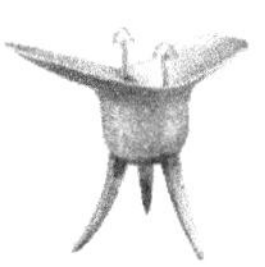

# ~85~

# 悔

刺，扎在心里
疼，却摸不着
——生发者早已远去

## *Regret*

*A thorn that pricks the heart constantly*
*Painful, yet untouchable*
*—— The one who caused it has long gone*

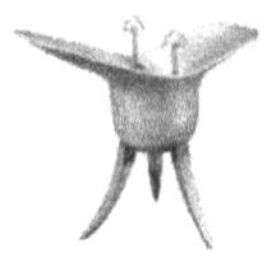

# ~*86*~

# 婚姻

水与火的历练
有时，火　气走了水
有时，水　冲走了火

## *Marriage*

*The trials of water and fire*
*At times, fire drives away the water*
*At times, water washes away the fire*

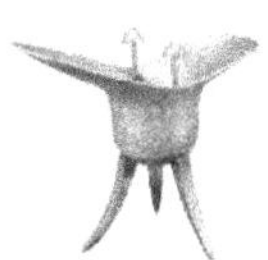

# ~*87*~

# 火（一）

心不空
岂能如此通透地
燃烧

## *Fire (I)*

*If its heart not empty*
*How can it burn*
*so brightly*

# ~88~

# 火（二）

送出的是光和热
留给自己的
是灰与冷

## *Fire (II)*

*To others, it gives light and warmth*
*To itself*
*Cold ashes*

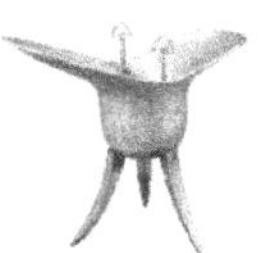

# ~*89*~

## 季节之恋

树林里，小屋慢慢露出头
风还未掸尽四下的落叶
月已勾大雁南去

### *The Love of the Season*

*In the woods, the little hut slowly emerges*
*While the wind has yet to sweep away the scattered leaves*
*The crescent moon has already drawn the wild geese southward*

# ~*90*~

## 桀骜自居

辽阔苍穹下
湖心一垂柳
顾影自怜

### *Proud Solitude*

*Under the vast blue sky*
*A weeping willow in the middle of the lake*
*Admires its own refection*

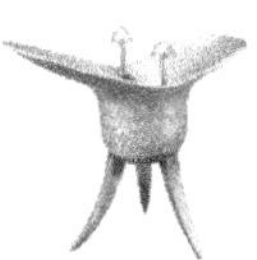

# ~*91*~

家

白雪
黑伞
朝迷蒙深处的炊烟游动

## **Home**

*White snow*
*A black umbrella*
*Drifting toward the cooking smoke curling in the deep mist*

# ~92~

# 教堂

虔诚并不够
还得符合物理原理
要不，为何都造一个高高的尖顶

## Church

*Piety alone won't suffice*
*Following the laws of physics is essential too*
*Otherwise, why would each erect a towering spire atop the roof*

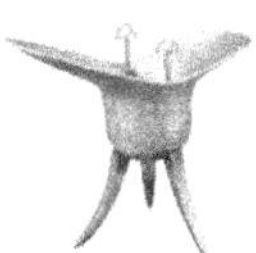

# ~93~

# 街灯

世态万千
越看
越昏黄

## Street Lamp

*The world is in vicissitudes*
*The more the watch*
*The more it dims*

# ~94~

## 晶莹的玻璃

浑浊硅砂的
浴火
重生

### Crystal Clear Glass

*The rebirth*
*From the turbid silica sand*
*Through the baptism of fire*

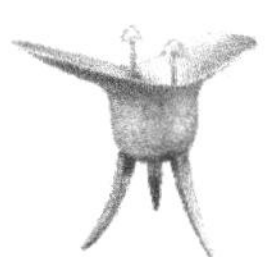

# ~95~

## 净心

枭雄弄潮

渔樵煮酒

都躲不过浪花

### Purifying the Heart

*Mighty leaders, wave riders*
*Fishermen and woodcutters, revelers in wine*
*None can evade the splashing waves*

# ~96~

# 九寨沟

沟沟
是
勾

## *Jiuzhaigou*

*Vale, vale**
*Each*
*Is an call*

Note *The Chinese word* 沟 *(gōu, meaning valley or vale) is homophonic to* 勾 *(gōu, meaning to hook or to call). Through the wordplay from* 沟 *to* 勾*, the Chinese poem explores the theme of why Jiuzhaigou, the famous valley, is so appealing.*

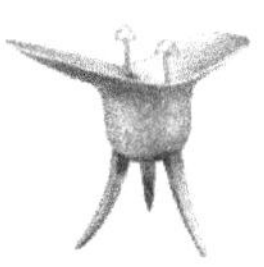

# ~97~

# 酒（一）

百慕达
表面平静喜庆
多少高飞的都坠失其中

## *Alcohol (I)*

*Bermuda*
*Surface calm and festive*
*Yet many soaring aspirations are lost within*

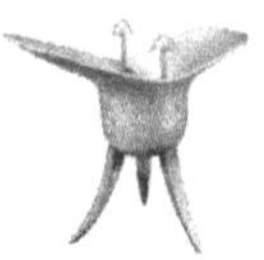

# ~98~

# 酒（二）

黑白两道通吃
黑　以肉与色为友
白　与诗人和英雄结交

## *Alcohol (II)*

*Straddles both black and white domains**
*Black, befriending flesh and desire*
*White, mingling with poets and heroes*

*Note In Chinese, the phrase "black and white paths" typically symbolizes the contrast between legitimate and illicit societal forces.*

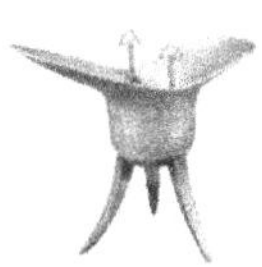

# ~*99*~

# 酒（三）

一杯又一杯
杯杯含着泪
恋她太心累　不如恋上你

## **Alcohol (III)**

*Glass after glass*
*Each holding unshed tears*
*Loving her weighs so heavy; Better to fall in love with you*

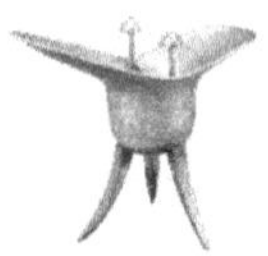

# ~100~

## 酒杯

一杯接一杯　杯杯带咸味
是里面滴进了我的泪
还是里面看见了你的影

### The Wine Cup

*Cup after cup, each tastes salty*
*Have my tears dripped in*
*or have I seen your reflection?*

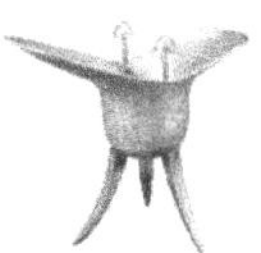

# ~101~

# 眷恋

那不经意的回眸一瞥
像睡莲落座心湖
时不时晃出涟漪

## Longing

*That inadvertent glance over the shoulder*
*Like a water lily settling on the heart's lake*
*Rippling out waves from time to time*

# ~102~

## 渴望

雪野
一只缩颈白鹭
呆望着冰封的河溪，等待——

### Longing

*In the snowy wilderness*
*A heron with its neck withdrawn*
*Looks at the frozen creek, waiting ——*

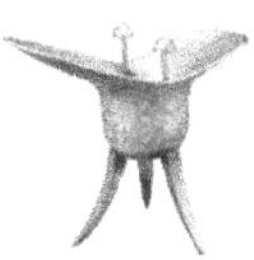

# ~103~

## 空竹

做空
抛出去
才能溜溜扯转，哗哗扯响

### *Diabolo*

*Make it empty**
*Cast it out*
*Only then can it spin and twirl, resonating with a lucrative hum*

Note The Chinese expression 做空 *(zuò kòng) has a dual meanings, making it a wordplay. As a financial term, it means "short-selling," while in a non-financial context, it means "to make empty," referring to making the diabolo hollow.*

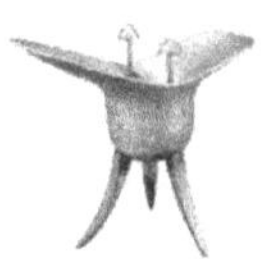

# ~104~

## 快递小哥

为解家这道题
他叠起方方的，顺着长长的
用圆圆的圈转出一个个几何图形


**The Delivery Guy**

*To solve this family problem*
*He stacks the square ones, follows the long ones*
*And uses the round ones to draw out various geometric shapes*

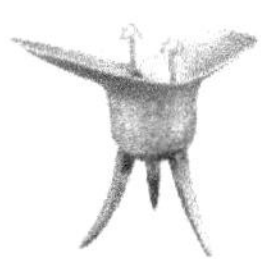

# ~105~

# 狂草

有一种激情
唯有龙腾虎跃、鸾翔凤舞
方能淋漓表达

## *Wild Cursive Script*

*There is such a passion*
*Only when dragons soar, tigers leap, phoenixes dance*
*Can thoroughly express*

# ~106~

## 喇叭花

一大早　就直立院墙上晃动婀娜身躯
直播时光主题曲
直到黄昏才躬身谢幕而眠

### The Morning Glory

*Early in the morning, it stands on the courtyard wall, swaying gracefully*
*Broadcasting the theme song of time*
*Until dusk falls, when it bows and retires to sleep*

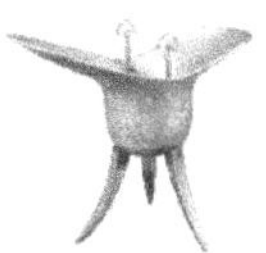

# ~*107*~

# 老农

一把锄头
硬是把太阳从东边拽到西边
然后掮着月牙下山

## *An Old Farmer*

*With a hoe in hand*
*He pulls the sun from east to west*
*Then shoulders the crescent moon downhill*

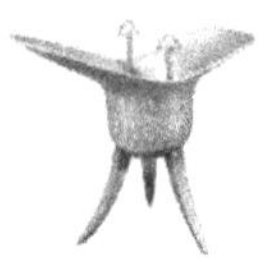

# ~108~

# 老墙根

早已闲得苔绿
那块滑弹砖*
斑驳着童年的故事　在暖阳里瞌睡

### The Foot of the Old Wall

*Long at rest, now covered in green moss*
*That glass-ball-rolling brick*
*Mottled with childhood tales, dozes in the warm sunshine*

*Note:* "滑弹砖"，又名"笃弹砖"，上海方言，用来让孩子们把弹子扔在上面让其滚远的砖头。

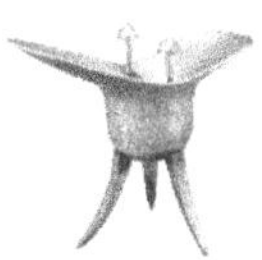

# ~109~

# 老樟树

遍体的伤
攀登九霄的天途中
留下的

## The Old Camphor Tree

*Scars all over its body*
*Marks it bore*
*While climbing the sky*

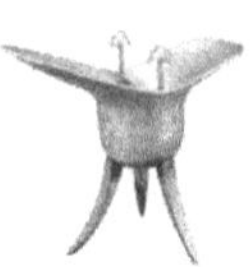

# ~110~

浪

江水的
心
思

**Waves**

*The Longing
of
Waters*

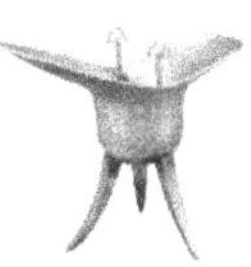

# ~111~

## 浪淘沙

人
物
史

### Waves Washing the Sand*

*The history
Of
Figures*

Note: *The title "Waves Washing the Sand" comes from the Chinese* 浪淘沙, *which is the name of a classical Chinese Ci poem format, popular during the Song Dynasty.*

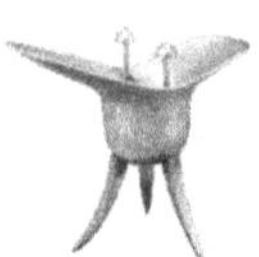

# ~112~

## 犁

父亲的背
哪一朵泥花
不是弓着身开出

### The Plow

*Father's back-----*
*Which soil flower*
*Doesn't bloom with his back arched?*

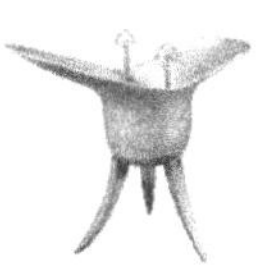

# ~113~

## 灵感

核仁形云层里迸出一道闪电
无数惊马从高山、林莽......
奔向诗的远方

### Inspiration

*From the kernel-shaped cloud bursts forth lightning*
*Countless startled steeds, from high mountains and dense forests...*
*Galloping toward the distant realms of poetry*

# ~114~

# 柳

斗笔　蘸长空青墨
在池帛上挥毫季画
云游　芦摇　燕飞　鱼翔……

## *Willow*

*A grand brush dips into the blue ink of the vast sky*
*Splashing spring images on the silk scroll of the pond:*
*Roaming clouds, swaying reeds, darting swallows, gliding fish..*

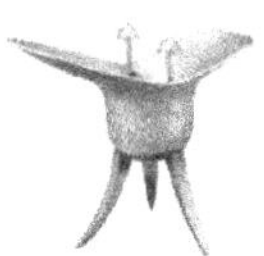

# ~115~

# 流水

真地无情？
看那垂柳轻抚荡起的
阵阵涟漪

## **Running Water**

*Truly heartless?*
*Look at the ripples*
*Stirred up by the soft touch of the willow*

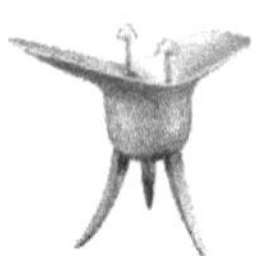

# ~116~

# 笼

现成的水　现成的食
打开它
鸟为何还是一冲而出？

## *Cage*

*Water and food, all prepared*
*Opening the door*
*Why does the bird still dash out?*

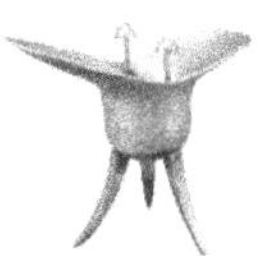

# ~117~

# 路

父亲走过的路
都粗犷地深刻在他的额上
不愿遗传给我们

## **The Road**

*Father has walked
Roughly etched upon his brow
He doesn't want to pass it down to us*

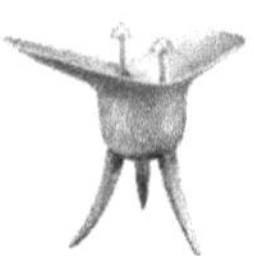

# ~118~

## 芦花

脚　陷在泥塘里
头　也要高扬
趴下　就再难飞起

### Reed Flowers

*Feet sink into the muddy pond*
*But the head must still rise high*
*For once you lie down, you can never fly again*

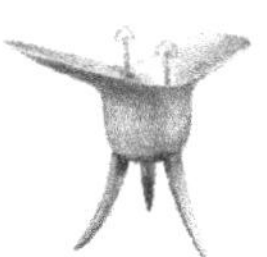

# ~119~

## 芦苇

顶戴花翎
高高地仰着头
水在它脚下默不作声

### Reed

*Crowned with a peacock's plume*
*Proudly held aloft*
*Yet the water at its feet remains silent*

# ~120~

## 论文

西人把它称作"纸"
难道其中很多
不是纸吗

### *Essay*

*Westerners term it "paper"*
*Aren't many of them*
*After all, just paper?*

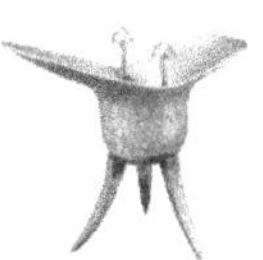

## ~121~

# 落叶

满布的血丝隐约着
风雨经年的煎熬
但它并未卷曲　仍拼力起舞

### The Fallen Leaf

*Sprawling blood streaks vaguely reveal*
*The year's torment of wind and rain*
*Yet it remains uncurled, summoning all its strength to dance*

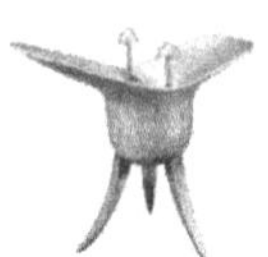

# ~122~

## 码头

水，哼着低沉的眠歌　瞌睡着
斜阳尽头
甚至没有一只报归海鸟

### Dock

*The water hums a low lullaby, drowsing…*
*At the end of the slanting sun*
*Not a single bird in sight, heralding a return*

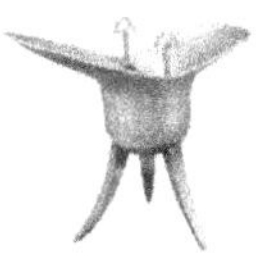

# ~123~

# 满江红

浴血史
壮观
不过弹指间

## Full River in Red*

*A history bathed in blood
Spectacular
Yet merely a snap of the fingers*

Note: The title "Full River in Red" comes from the Chinese 满江红, which is the name of a classical Chinese Ci poem format, popular during the Song Dynasty.

# ~124~

## 玫瑰

野蜂缠绕　蜻蜓撩拨
她仍双手托腮
昂首遥望

### *Rose*

*Wild bees entwine, dragonflies tease*
*Yet she cradles her cheeks with both hands*
*Gazing up, looking into the distance*

# ~125~

# 梅

知你，莫如雪
没它从九霄赶来
你还能火红地燃烧吗

### *Plum Blossom*

*In knowing you, nothing rivals snow*
*If it did not descend from the heavens*
*Would you still blaze with fiery crimson*

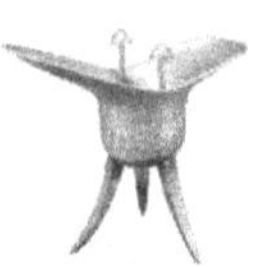

# ~126~

## 媒婆

柳倾身探水
溪仰面望柳
燕在其间传情

### A Matchmaker

*The willow bows to touch the creek*
*The creek gazes up at the willow*
*The swallow passes affection between them*

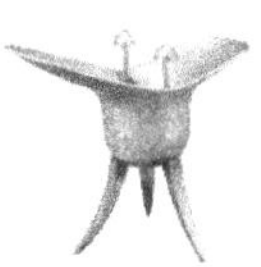

# ~127~

# 朦胧诗

云中
龙
爪

## **Misty Poetry**

*Dragon's
Claws
In clouds*

# ~128~

## 谜

风　一个侧翻由北转东
雪　一个趔趄戛然而止
难道只为让土拨鼠探头洞外？

## *Riddle*

*The wind, with a sudden flip, shifts from north to east*
*The snow, with an abrupt stumble, halts*
*All just to let the groundhog peek from its burrow?*

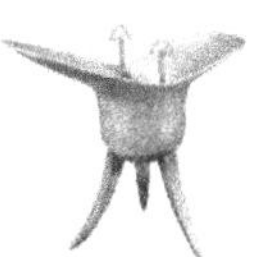

# ~129~

# 蜜蜂

花花世界里的
采蜜
高手

## The Bee

*A virtuoso in*
*Honey gathering*
*In the glamourous world of flowers*

# ~130~

淼

水
水
水

## Boundless Flood

*Water*
*Water*
*Water*

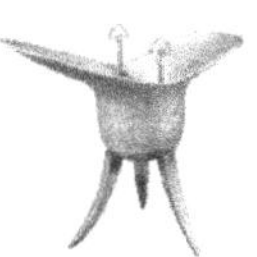

# ~131~

墨

深得莫测
潜入纸背
述说他的十年寒窗

**Ink**

*Deep and unfathomable*
*It dives into the paper's back*
*To tell the story of his ten years' diligence by the cold window*

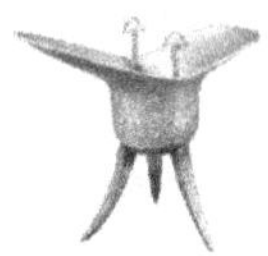

# ~132~

## 魔方

各执一面　互不相让
懂门道
才能在纷繁的世界里走出天地

### Rubik's Cube

*Each holds one side, refusing to yield*
*Only by understanding the way*
*Can one navigate a place in the chaos of the world*

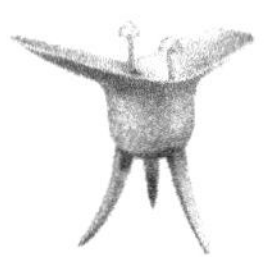

# ~133~

## 魔镜

如果只存在于童话
那你为什么有事
就敲它的窗子　向它虔诚地低头

### Magic Mirror

*If it exists only in fairy tales*
*Then why, when something happens*
*You knock on its window and bow to it devoutly?*

# ~134~

## 母亲端来的欢笑

热腾腾地
回响在饭桌上
萦绕全家

### The Laughter Mother Brought Over

*Steamy and lively*
*Echoes around the dinner table*
*Enveloping the entire family*

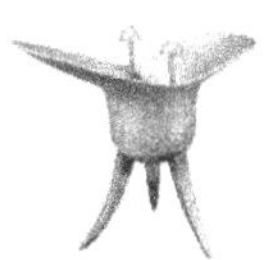

# ~135~

## 那株草

爬上了高墙
在风中孤独地左右逢源
它的兄弟们手牵着手蔓向远方

### *That Grass*

*Succeeds in climbing onto the high wall*
*Swaying alone in the wind to please both sides*
*Its brothers, hand in hand, spread into the distance*

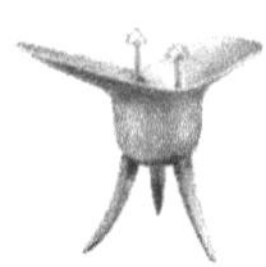

# ~136~

# 农夫山泉

谁说水往低处流?
我携着乡音
跑上了摩天大楼

**Nongfu Mountain Spring**

*Who says water flows downwards?*
*With hometown accent*
*I have climbed onto the skyscraper*

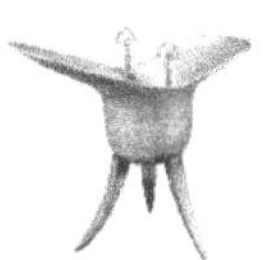

# ~*137*~

## 农夫

一担挑起一个家
爬山　涉水　熬寒　煎暑
都往田里赶

### *A Farmer*

*Shoulders the load of his family*
*Climbing mountains, wading waters, enduring cold, and sweltering heat*
*All to rush to the fields*

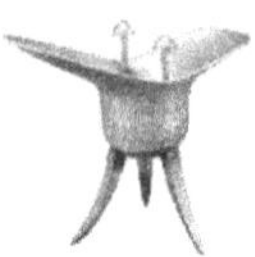

# ~138~

女儿红

几挂鞭炮　数巡行酒令
就划拉走了
家酿瑰宝

**The Daughter's Red***

*A few strings of firecrackers and a few rounds of drinking games*
*Quickly took away*
*The home-brewed treasure*

Note: The Daughter's Red is the translation of 女儿红 (nǚ ér hóng), a name of a well known Chinese wine.

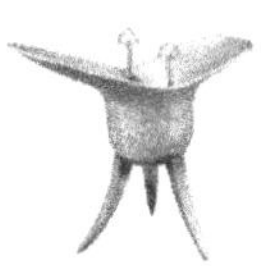

# ~139~

## 刨子

按下你就扒去一层皮
直到你厚薄如他意
光洁称他心

### *Plane*

*Pressing you down, it strips a layer of your skin*
*Until your thickness fits his will ——*
*Your smoothness pleases his eye*

# ~140~

## 盆景

铁丝
缠牵了他小小的生命轨迹
缠不住他揽天的宏愿

### *Bonsai*

*Iron wires*
*Bind it, guiding its small life's path*
*Yet cannot confine it from shaping the sky*

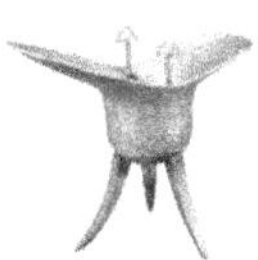

# ~141~

# 盆松

带着铁镣
飞
翔

## Pine Bonsai

Chained
Yet
Soars

# ~142~

# 喷泉

哪怕终会陨落
也要上天
灿烂一会

### **Fountain**

*Even if it will eventually fall*
*It must rise*
*To bloom brilliantly for a moment*

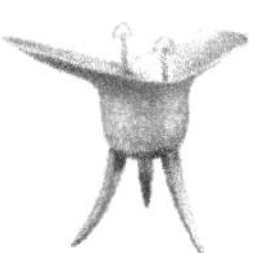

# ~143~

# 琵琶

弹指间
满盘
滴珠

## Pipa Musical Instrument

*Within snap of fingers*
*A full plate*
*Dripping pearls*

# ~144~

# 瀑布（一）

眺望远方的大海
毅然跃下
万丈峭壁

## *Waterfall (I)*

*Gazing at the distant sea*
*He boldly leaps down*
*From the sheer cliff of ten thousand feet*

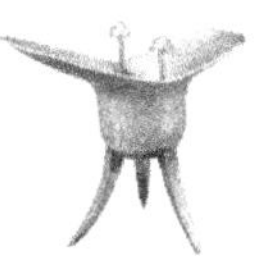

# ~145~

# 瀑布（二）

谁说没有龙
诺日朗下
它鳞光闪闪从云雾中轰鸣而来

## *Waterfall (II)*

*Who said dragons were mere myth*
*Under Nuorilang**
*It roars down from the clouds, scales shimmering*

*Note: Nuorilang is the widest travertine waterfall in China, standing at an elevation of 2,343 meters, with a height of 24.5 meters and a width of 320 meters. The roaring waters originate from the Nuorilang Plateau, echoing through the valley.*

# ~146~

# 蒲公英（一）

五月里举行的跳伞比赛
跳　是为了顺道定点
子女的未来

## Dandelion (I)

*A parachute jumping contest held in May*
*The jump also serves to pinpoint*
*The future of their children*

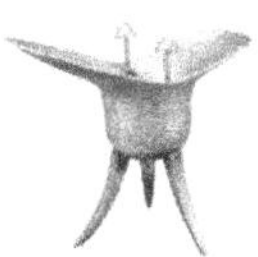

# ~147~

# 蒲公英（二）

一起风
就茫茫一片
忙着把子女送出山沟

## Dandelion (II)

*As soon as a gust of wind rises*
*They spread out in a vast stretch*
*Hastily sending their children out of the valley*

# ~148~

# 起风了

落叶飘飘然地说
"为何逆行？"
大江不答，朝东升旭日汹涌而去


## When Wind Rises

*The fallen leaves ask in a drifting tone*
*"Why go against the flow?"*
*The river gives no answer, but roars eastward, toward where the sun*
*rises*

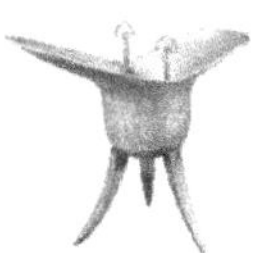

# ~149~

# 气根

突破土这位养父的束缚
结交信奉自由的气
独木成林

## *Aerial Roots*

*Breaking through the constraints of earth, the nurturing father*
*Forming bonds with the air, a believer in freedom*
*A single tree can become a forest*

# ~150~

## 气压锅

不停加火
一旦找到气口
当然怒气冲天，一涌而出

### The Pressure Cooker

*Continuously heating up*
*Once it finds an air outlet*
*Its anger will inevitably surge and burst out*

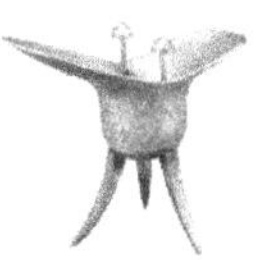



# 旗袍（一）

左襟搂右襟
母纽系公扣
打结处　情窦欲开的栀子花

## Cheongsam (I)

*Left lapel embraces right lapel*
*Female button fastens to the male button*
*At the knot, a passionate gardenia bud is about to bloom*

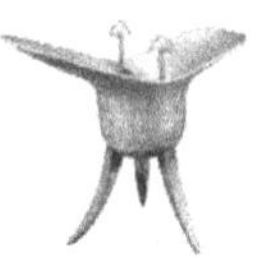

# ~152~

## 旗袍（二）

高衩处
若隐若现着
遐想


## Cheongsam (II)

*At the high slits*
*Floats*
*Many imaginations*

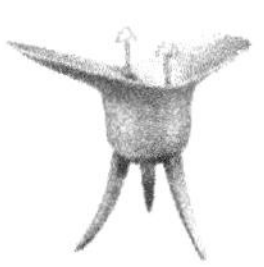

## *~153~*

# 旗袍（三）

和盘托出
一个民国式的江南女
走在短裙、肚兜，漏膝牛仔裤人群间

## *Cheongsam (III)*

*Projects*
*A Southern Republican-styled woman*
*Walking amidst the crowd in miniskirts, bellybands, and knee-revealing jeans*

# ~154~

## 旗袍（四）

拢着的是曲线
散发的是女性
透着的是江南

### *Cheongsam (IV)*

*Gathers curves*
*Radiates femininity*
*Pervades the charm of the south*

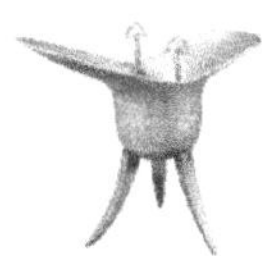

# ~155~

# 前线

火烧云低压着他渐小的背影
那里的隆隆声
隐约在她的心跳间

## The Frontline

*The burning clouds press his figure, diminishing into the distance*
*The rumbling sound from there*
*Faintly echoing in her heartbeat*

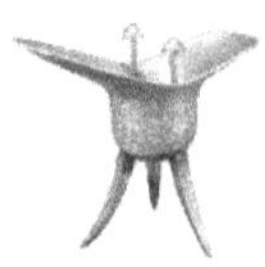

# ~156~

# 青花瓷（一）

历经深土里黑暗的磨砺
历经泥窑里烈火的锻造
方才与青天齐名

## Blue and White Porcelain (I)

*Enduring the dark refinement in the deep earth*
*Forged in the intense fire of the kiln*
*Only then does it stand equal to the blue sky*

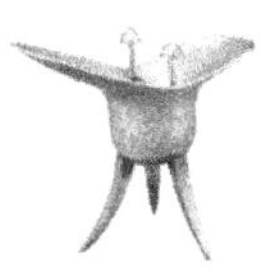

# ~157~

# 青花瓷（二）

是谁色诱青天
落入皇宫贵府、还有小巷民宅
把难以兑现的公正精神　寄托在花瓶上

## Blue and White Porcelain (II)

*Who tempted the blue sky*
*Into royal palaces, noble estates, and humble alleyways*
*Placing the unfulfilled spirit of justice in the vase*

# ~158~

# 情到深处

一对白天鹅交颈
羞红
满湖的晚霞

## When Emotions Run Deep

*Entwined their necks in love's embrace, two white swans*
*Blush*
*The lake with fiery evening clouds*

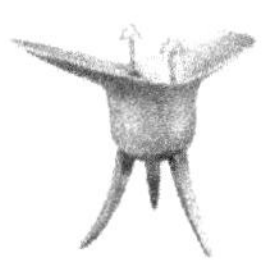

# ~159~

## 蜻蜓

远道驾机来向荷花表白
受到冷遇也悬而不舍
形成一道追星的亮丽风景

### Dragonfly

*Flying from afar to confess to the lotus*
*Met with indifference, yet still hanging on*
*Creating a stunning scene in pursuit of stars*

# ~160~

## 情网

一个
陷
阱

**Love Web**

*A*
*Tangled*
*Snare*

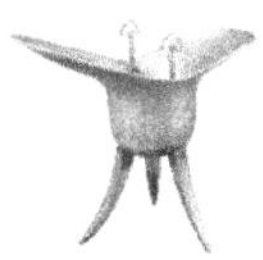

# ~161~

# 情在深处

朦胧烟雨渲染
粉墙黛瓦写意
拱桥上油纸伞眺望远方的留白

## Where Passion Lies Deep

*Misty drizzle, rendered for an aura*
*Black roof tiles and white walls, arranged for impression*
*The paper umbrella atop the arched bridge gazes into the distant*
*blank space*

# ~162~

桥

水
上
丰　碑

## *Bridge*

*a*
*Monument*
*On water*

# ~163~

# 秋（一）

潘多拉魔盒
满装绚丽的色之宝藏
我知不能贪婪，却克服不了色诱

## Autumn (I)

*Pandora's Box*
*Filled with a treasure of dazzling colors*
*I know I mustn't be greedy, yet I cannot escape its lure*

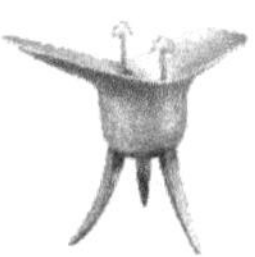

# ~164~

# 秋（二）

马良为山乡绘画
红日、赤霞、黄枫……
还有遍地金色稻谷

### Autumn (II)

*P Ma Liang* paints for the mountain village*
*Red sun, crimson clouds, yellow maples...*
*And golden rice fields everywhere*

*Note: Ma Liang is a painter from a Chinese fairy tale. He has a magical brush, and whatever he paints becomes real. He is kind-hearted and often paints for the common people.*

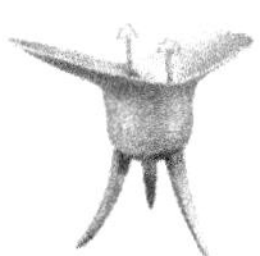

# ~165~

## 秋（三）

谁，打开了炉膛
要不，为何满眼
火红

### *Autumn (III)*

*Who opened the furnace?*
*Or else, why are my eyes filled*
*with blazing red?*

# ~166~

## 秋风

定然起自炉膛
要不，漫山遍野的枫树
为何烧得火样红

### Autumn Wind

*Must rise from a furnace*
*If not, why is the mountain covered with*
*Flaming red maple trees*

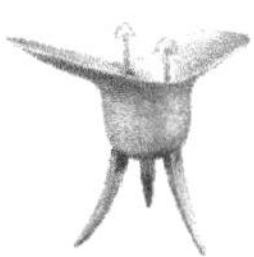

# ~167~

秋色

浓烈的黄酒
一呷
就醉

## Autumn's Color

*Strong yellow wine*
*One sip*
*Instant intoxication*

# ~168~

## 秋声

蝉鸣　蛙歌　蛐叫……
协奏曲
激我侧耳向东

### The Autumn Sounds

*The chirping of cicadas, the song of frogs, the call of crickets...*
*A concerto*
*Urging me to turn my ear to the east*

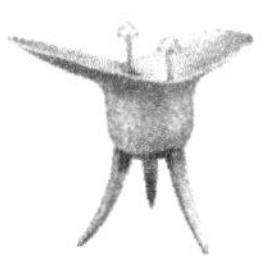

# ~169~

# 秋叶（一）

年轻时斑斓的梦
高挂在树干上炫耀一阵后
就纷纷坠落了

## Autumn Leaves (I)

*The colorful dreams of youth*
*Hung high on the tree trunk, flaunting for a while*
*Then fell one by one*

# ~170~

# 秋叶（二）

辉煌后
伴着风鸣的安魂曲
飘向无垠

## Autumn Leaves (II)

*After their brilliance fades*
*Amidst the requiem of the wind*
*They drift into the boundless expanse*

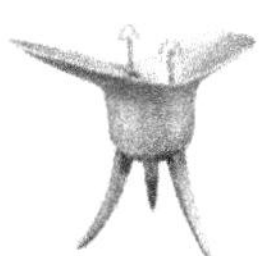

# ~171~

秋千

一次次上跃
总因牵挂
而折回

## The Swing

*Soars up time and again*
*But always returns*
*Because of attachment*

# ~172~

## 求索

阴沉的天空下
寒冷的雪岩上
一支瘦梅　仍在翘首燃烧

### The Quest

*Beneath the gloomy sky*
*Upon the cold, snowy rocks*
*A slender plum, still lifts its head, burning brightly*

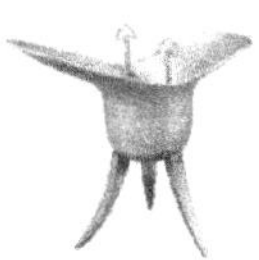

# ~*173*~

## 缺席的时空

把襁褓凝固在视窗里
让缺席的记忆
在未来返回席位

### *The Absence of Time and Space*

*Freeze the swaddled infant in the window's view*
*To let the absent memory*
*Return to its seat in the future*

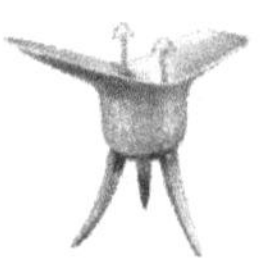

## ~174~

人

一辈子都在赶
车上　键盘上　甚至吃饭……
赶着赶着　就到了点

**A Person**

*Bustles through life
On the bus, at the keyboard, even while eating...
Rushing and rushing, then, abruptly, it's over*

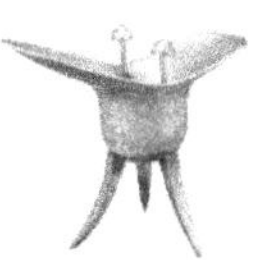

# ~175~

## 人生

一粒向西而飘的微尘
身不由己，不知落点，不知落时
那就飘逸吧

## *Life*

*A mere speck of dust drifting westward*
*Unable to control itself, unaware of where or when it will land*
*So, why not float gracefully*

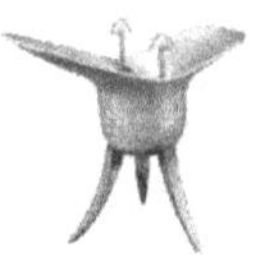

# ~176~

## 人生抉择

背阳路
才会走在
阴影里

### The Choice of Life

*Take the path with the sun behind*
*And you will walk*
*In the shadows*

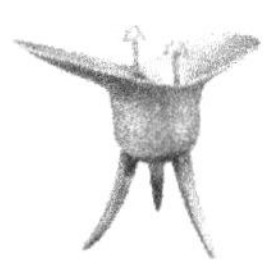

## ~177~

人生憾事溪与柳

近在咫尺却
水　空流而走
絮　空飞而去

**Regrets in Life: The Stream and the Willow**

*So near, yet*
*The water can only flow away on its own*
*The catkins can only drift away in solitude*

# ~178~

# 仁爱河

我是一条船
无论急行缓淌
都行不出母亲开凿的河

## A River of Benevolence

*I am a boat*
*Swift or slow my ride*
*I cannot depart from the river Mother excavated*

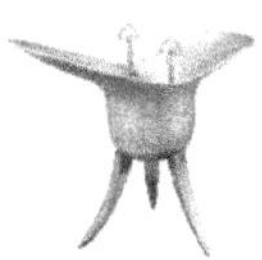

# ~179~

# 赛事

一个激灵
无数蝌蚪激流勇往
竞争，从跃入新世界前就已开始

## The Race

*A sudden thrill*
*Countless tadpoles brave the rapids*
*Competition begins long before reaching the springboard to a new*
*world*

# ~*180*~

# 三行诗

一行是盆
二行是植
三行是蓝天

## *A Three-Line Poem*

*One line is the pot*
*The second is the plant*
*The third is the blue sky*

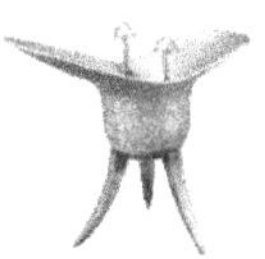

# ~181~

# 三角粽

棱棱角角
每一个
都勾股着遥远故乡的边

## *Triangular Zongzi*

*Edges and corners*
*Each one*
*Squares the distant borders of my hometown*

# ~182~

## 森林

同在一片闰土
哪棵不是翘首望天
却为何仍参差不齐

### *Forest*

*Living together in the same fertile soil*
*Which tree does not crane toward the sky?*
*Why, then, this irregularity?*

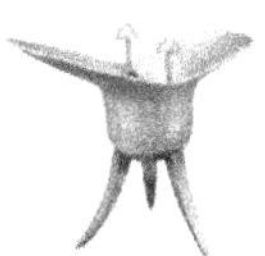

# ~183~

# 沙漏（一）

你在红尘里的
上下左右
定位于上一个轮回

## *Hourglass (I)*

*In this mundane world*
*Up, down, left, right*
*You are positioned in the previous cycle*

# ~184~

# 沙漏（二）

一个置身其中
就无法止步的大千
直到陨落

## Hourglass (II)

*The boundless universe*
*Once inside, there's no stopping*
*Until the fall*

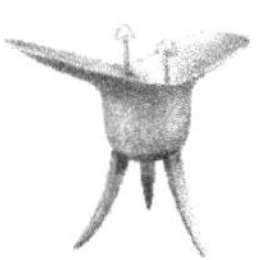

# ~185~

# 沙漏（三）

漏下
就无法回天
直到上帝之手重置乾坤

## Hourglass (III)

*Once trickles down*
*No turning back until*
*The hand of God resets the universe*

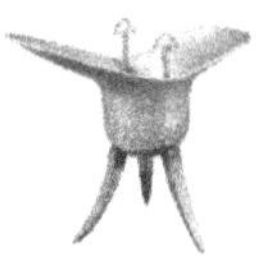

# ~*186*~

## 擅思

起于溪
涌入河
汇成大海，兴风作浪

### *Good Thinking*

*Begins in a stream*
*Flows into the river*
*Merges into the ocean, stirring winds and waves*

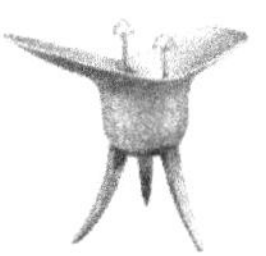

# ~*187*~

山

出生地壳深处
却撼地而出冲天而起
用陡峰峭壁勾勒天的意志

## **Mountain**

*Born deep within the earth's crust*
*Yet it shakes the ground and rises to the sky*
*Outlining the will of the heavens with its steep peaks and cliffs*

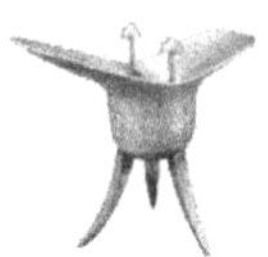

# ~188~

## 山谷

头顶，云忙着作秀
四周，峰自顾傲视
我敞怀拥抱一切投身者

### *Valley*

*Above, the clouds busy showing off*
*Around, peaks aloof and self-assured*
*I embrace wholeheartedly all who venture here*

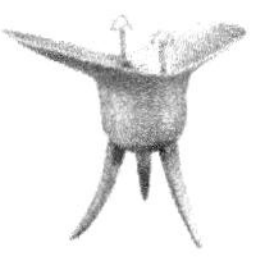

# ~189~

## 山月

从老家走来
带着我童年憧憬的玉兔与嫦娥
守在我窗前不肯离去

### Mountain Moon

*Comes from my hometown,*
*Carrying the jade rabbit and Chang'e lady of my childhood dreams,*
*Lingering by my window, unwilling to leave*

*Note: In Chinese mythology, Chang'e is the Moon Goddess, who lives on the moon after consuming an immortality elixir. Her companion, the Jade Rabbit, is said to reside with her, continuously pounding herbs to make the elixir.*

# ~190~

# 山泉

出生穷乡
闭关深岩练就的本领
把它送进了摩天大楼

## Mountain Spring

*Born in a humble village*
*Yet the skills refined in deep secluded rocks*
*Sends it into skyscrapers*

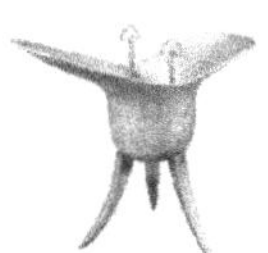

# ~191~

## 山与河

不知是河缠山
还是山护着河
总之　它俩在一起是道亮丽风景

### Mountain and River

*Not sure if the river winds around the mountain*
*Or the mountain shields the river*
*Regardless, their union creates a splendid landscape*

# *~192~*

## 陕北民歌

高

高

每一声都　直飙　黄土高坡

### ***Shaanbei Folk Song***

*High*
*High*
*Each sound soars straight onto the Loess Plateau*

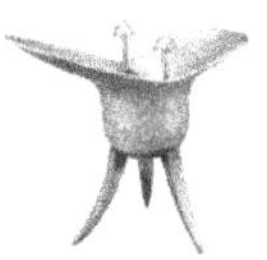

# ~193~

## 少妇

楼窗后
夜夜叹月远
今夜雪霁　又怨月太近

### The Young Woman

*Behind the window of a storied house*
*Nightly sighs at the distant moon*
*Tonight, after the snow clears, she bemoans its closeness*

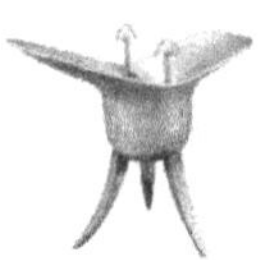

# ~194~

## 谁？

驴，磨，主人
谁转了一辈子圈
没有走出来?

## *Who?*

*The donkey, the millstone, and the master*
*Who has spent a lifetime turning in circles*
*Without ever stepping out?*

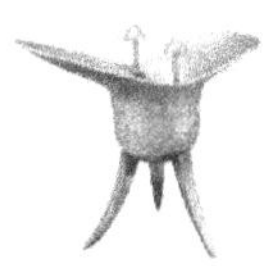

# ~195~

## 谁把春天藏了起来

几只小鸟
用爪
在雪地上到处扒拉

## Who Has Hidden Away Spring

*A few small birds*
*Probe with their claws*
*Everywhere in the snowy ground*

# ~196~

# 嗜酒

喝下的酒如未被身体吸收
肯定泛滥成河
好在它被身体吸收了

## **Alcohol Craving**

*If the alcohol you drink were not absorbed by your body*
*It would surely flood into a river*
*Fortunately, your body has absorbed it*

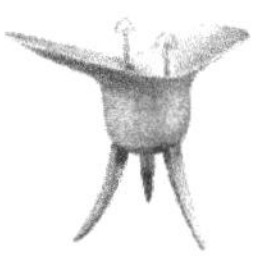



# 诗

一把测试
思维与情感深度与广度的
尺

## **Poetry**

*A measure
of the depth and breadth
of thought and emotion*

## ~198~

# 诗和远方

他们说　云里有诗
我端详许久也没找到
却被它不知不觉带到远方

## Poetry and Distance

*They say within clouds resides poetry*
*I gaze at them intently, but find none*
*Yet unwittingly, they carry me to distant realms*

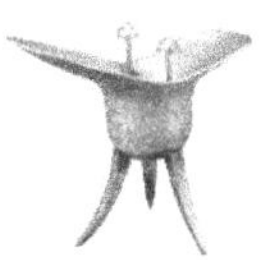

# ~199~

## 诗界

一跂跌入　坐看
群山争峰
众川争流

**The Realm of Poetry**

*Stumbling in, seated to watch*
*Mountains vie for peaks*
*Rivers vie for currents*

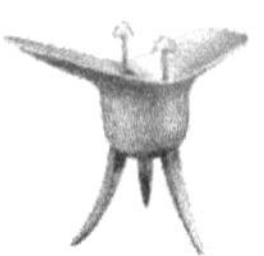

# ~200~

## 时间（一）

把它敲进键盘
打印出来
化作墨香飘逸

### Time (I)

*Tap it into the keyboard*
*Print it out*
*And let the ink's fragrance spread*

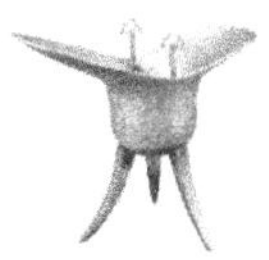

# ~*201*~

# 时间（二）

驮着你不停地跑
直到你被颠得喘不过气
从它身上摔下来

## *Time (II)*

*Carries you relentlessly*
*Running until you're breathless*
*And thrown off*

# ~202~

# 时风

西域刮来一阵风
卷走
一半并蒂莲

## The Temporal Wind

*From the Western lands*
*Whisks away*
*One of the paired lotus blooms*

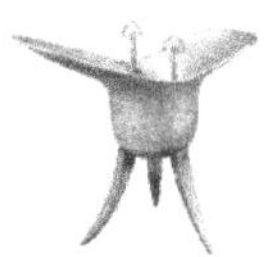

# ~203~

# 书签

独步天下
在路的尽头
跃入另一个世界

## Bookmark

*A solitary traveler in the world*
*At the end of the road*
*Leaps into another realm*

# ~204~

## 说是有情却无情

起风了
柳一甩青丝
凭溪水无情远去

**Love Is Said to Be Affectionate, Yet Seems Heartless**

*When the wind rises*
*The willow tosses its verdant strands aside*
*While the creek indifferently gurgles into the distance*

# ~205~

四季

风水轮流转*
和、熏、金、朔
都有风头出

**Four Seasons**

*The tide turns,*
*Gentle breeze, warm breeze, autumn wind, and north wind,*
*Each has its time to shine*

"风水轮流转" *(fēng shuǐ lún liú zhuǎn) is a Chinese proverb, which suggests that fortune or circumstances change in turn.*

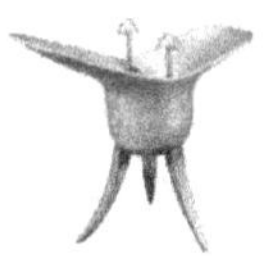

# ~206~

## 思念

是一枚
插在心房里的红豆枝
汲我脉动的血日夜生长

**Longing**

*Is a*
*Red bean sprout nestled in my heart*
*Drawing from my pulsing blood, growing day and night*

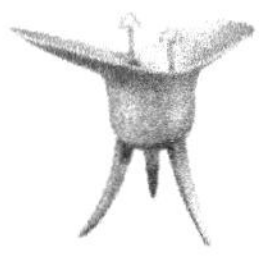

# ~207~

思之旅

一手托起鲲
一手掀动鹏翅
乘着它　傲游星空海角

## A Journey of Thought

*Holding up Kun* with one hand*
*Flapping the wings of Peng* with the other*
*Riding it, I travel to starry skies and vast oceans*

*Note: According to Chinese philosopher Zhuangzi's "Free & Easy Wandering," the Kunpeng has an enormous form. Whether it is in the shape of the fish Kun or the form of bird Peng, its size is said to stretch for thousands of miles.*

# ~208~


水


上　居九天
下　潜深壑
呼啦啦的风　喜上而少下


## Water


*Above, it dwells in the nine heavens*
*Below, it plunges into deep ravines*
*The howling wind likes to ascend, but seldom descends*

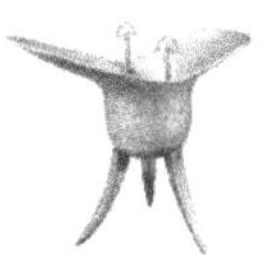

# ~*209*~

# 水与酒

投胎技术决定命运
一个坠入土罐泥杯
一个荣入金樽玉爵

## **Water and Wine**

*The technique of rebirth decides fate*
*One falls into an earthen jar or a clay cup*
*The other into a golden goblet or a jade vessel*

# ~*210*~

# 岁月

驱走了
我童年时
圈养在云海里的宠物

## *Time*

*Has driven away*
*The pets I once kept*
*In the sea of clouds during my childhood*

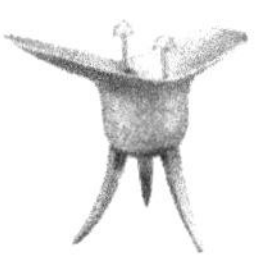

# ~211~

## 笋

顶出脑尖　支起耳瓣
跐直一节节身子
看四下的立体春景视频

**Bamboo Shoot**

*Pushing through the tip of its head, lifting its earlobes*
*Each segment straightening on tiptoe*
*It gazes at the 3D video of the spring scenery around it*

# ~212~

## 蒜球

合家欢
靠的就是
那根顶梁柱

## Garlic Bulb

*Family Joy*
*All relies on*
*That central pillar*

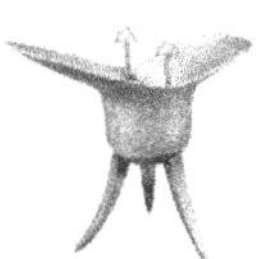

# ~213~

## 她 的 心

西　沉　月

### *Her Heart*

*Crescent moon*
　　　　*Sinking*
*to the west*

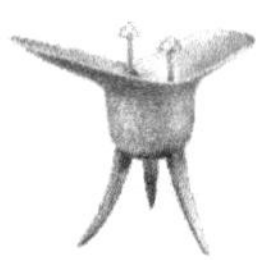

# ~214~

# 昙花

睁开花的明眸
看到这世界满尘
当天就闭了

## *The Fleeting Flower*

*Opening its bright floral eyes*
*It sees a world full of dust*
*And closes them that very day*

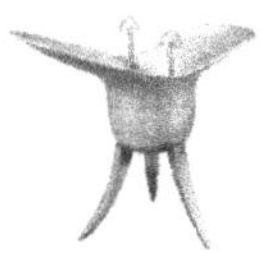

# ~215~

## 糖

果真是一种有机化合物
有了它　再差的关系
也会化合得甜起来

### *Sugar*

*Indeed, an organic compound*
*With which, even the poorest relations*
*Can be compounded to sweeten up a bliss*

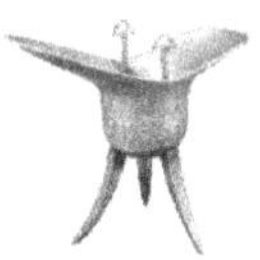

# ~216~

## 桃花

谢红数度
一旁暗情井水依旧羞却无声
风来了　卷起落瓣它去

**Peach Blossoms**

*Have fallen several times*
*While the nearby well water remains quietly shy, hiding its feelings*
*The wind comes and rolls the petals away*

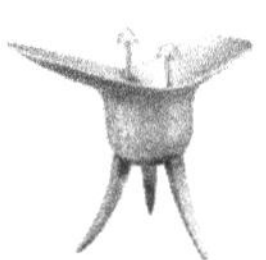

# ~217~

## 腾挪

把令人见之悚然的鳄鱼的皮
挂在女士肩下
立马就悦人眼球

### *Shifting*

*Drape a fearsome crocodile hide*
*Beneath a lady's shoulder*
*Instantly, it captivates the eye*

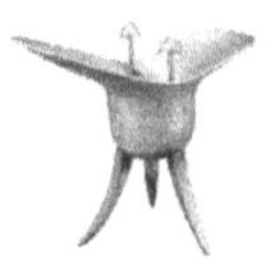

# ~218~

## 听雪

白雪、黑伞、一对偎依的背影
扑簌簌的
是雪声还是心跳

### Listening to Snowfall

*White snow, a black umbrella, the backsight of two leaning figures*
*Is the soft patter*
*The sound of snow or their heartbeats*

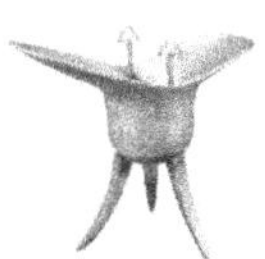

# ~219~

## 童话世界

嫦娥朝窗外拂一袖寒风
漫天星斗眨眨眼
晃悠悠从天而降

### The Realm of Fairy Tales

*Lady Chang'e flicks a sleeve of cold wind out the window*
*A skyful of stars twinkling and winking*
*Swaying gently down from the heavens*

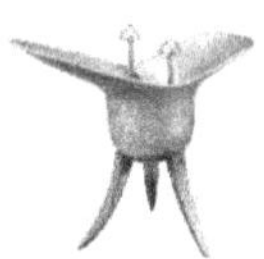

# ~220~

## 铜铃的抉择

投靠筹捐者，舒适地乞讨
追随骑驼人
艰辛，但穿越沙漠

### The Bell's Dilemma

*Joining fundraisers, comfortably begging*
*Following a camel rider*
*Challenging, yet crossing deserts*

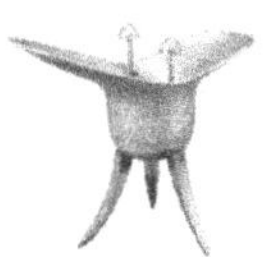

# ~221~

## 突来的雪

扑簌簌地落
一只土拨鼠到处乱窜
急着寻找回家的路

**The Sudden Snow**

*Thuds down*
*A groundhog scurries everywhere*
*Rushing to find its way home*

# ~222~

## 驼铃

再小
打破的是沉寂 穿越的是无垠
摇响它的是一个高大的身影

### The Camel Bell

*However tiny*
*It breaks silence and crosses the vastness*
*Shaking it is a lofty figure*

# ~223~

## 陀螺（一）

鞭笞何惧
挺直了
才能凯旋

## Spinning Top (I)

*Fear no lashes*
*Only when stand up*
*Can I triumph*

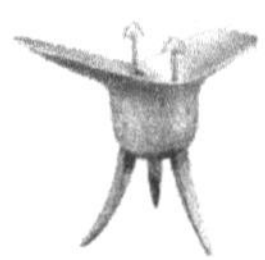

# ~224~

## 陀螺（二）

父亲　不停地抽
每一抽
都是爱


## *The Spinning Top (II)*

*Father never stops whipping*
*Each whip*
*Is love*

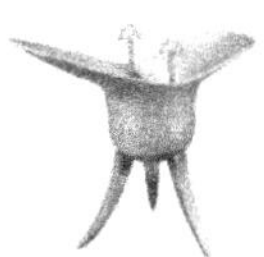

# ~225~

# 望天树

生性莫不作声
只顾汲取养分
才冲入云霄

## Parashorea Chinensis

*Born silent*
*Yet focused on absorbing nutrients*
*It now soars into the clouds*

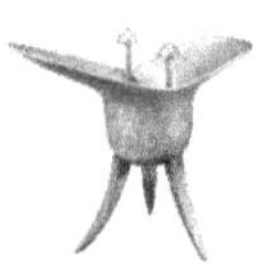

# ~226~

## 网络

纵横交错
从里朝外看　呈现的是世界
从外朝里看　网住的是心灵

### *The Web*

*Interwoven*
*Gazing outward from within, a world unfolds*
*Looking inward from without, it frames the heart and mind*

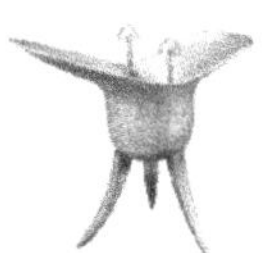

# ~227~

# 往事（一）

都浮雕在
父亲满掌的老茧上
难以退却

## *The Past (I)*

*All etched in relief*
*On father's callused palms*
*Hard to erase*

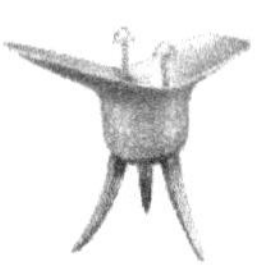

# ~228~

# 往事（二）

飘渺
疼在难以捕捉
却越要捕捉

## The Past (II)

*Elusive*
*The more painful it is to capture them*
*The more determined we are to do so*

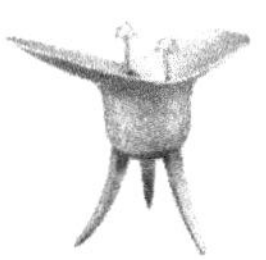

# ~229~

## 微诗

挥动心剑
截断冰川　推入大海
把生命的源藏在冰尖下

### Micro-Poems

*Swinging the sword within my heart's grasp*
*I sever glaciers, nudging them into the vast sea*
*Concealing the wellspring of life beneath the tip of ice*

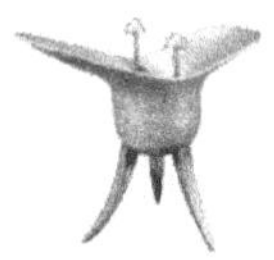

# ~230~

## 我的诗

无需长江那么长
却像它那样深邃湍急
映着天空、高山、林莽……

### My Poems

*Need not be as lengthy as the Yangtze River*
*Yet as deep and torrential*
*Filled with skies, high mountains, dense forests...*

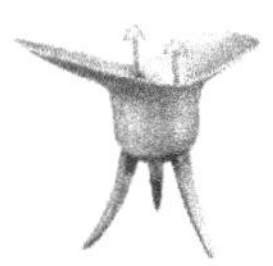

# ~231~

## 我的河

爱它　不是因为它深邃流长
是因为
它心里装着一片蓝天

### **My River**

*I cherish it not because of its depth or length*
*But because*
*It lies within my heart a piece of the blue sky*

# ~232~

## 钨丝

凭你锁骨、通电、燎烤
我仍要把光明
送给人间

### Tungsten Filament

*Despite clasp, electrify, and scorch*
*I persist in bringing light*
*To the human world*

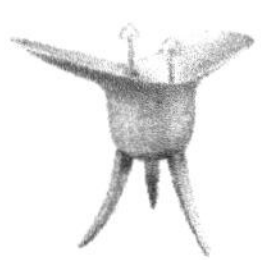

# ~233~

## 雾

晨风
催生了
一个车水马龙的城市

## *Fog*

*The morning breeze*
*Brings to life*
*A bustling city*

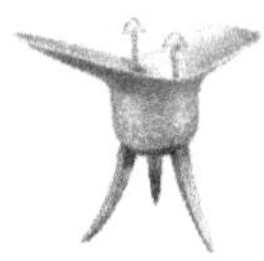

# ~234~

# 乌云

伸开了手
太阳硬是从它的指缝间
洒下万道金光

## The Dark Clouds

*Stretch out their hands*
*The sun forces its way through their fingers*
*Cascading myriad rays of golden light*

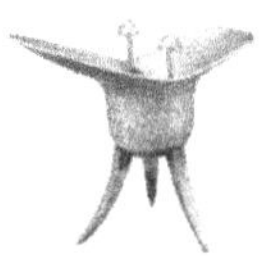

# ~235~

# 乌龟

长寿的秘诀是
每次缩头都是心火
在生命水银柱上的减势

## *A Tortoise*

*The secret of its longevity is*
*Every time it retracts its head, its heart fire*
*Subsides along the mercury column of life*

# ~236~

## 无题

云的高度雨知道
人的厚重
风晓得

### *Untitled*

*The height of the clouds, rain knows*
*A man's weight*
*The wind*

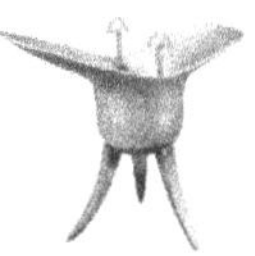

# ~237~

## 喜讯

硕大旭日前
一阵耳语后
蝴蝶扭起了秧歌，稻穗晃起了伦巴

### Happy Tidings

*Before the gigantic morning sun*
*After a gentle whisper*
*The butterflies began to dance the yangge*, the rice ears swayed to*
*the rumba*

*Note: Yangge is a traditional Chinese folk dance, often performed during festivals. It features lively, rhythmic movements accompanied by drumming and lively music. Dancers, usually in vibrant costumes, use props like fans or flags, embodying joy, energy, and community spirit. It has roots in agricultural celebrations.*

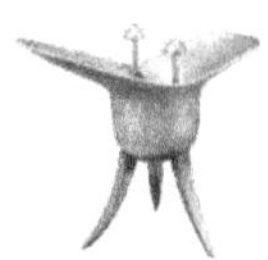

# ~238~

# 夕阳（一）

火红的句号
句住又一个丰硕
跃向另一个辉煌

## Sunset (I)

*A fiery red period*
*Marking the end of another fruitful day*
*Leaping toward yet another brilliance*

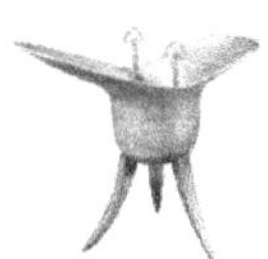

# ~239~

# 夕阳（二）

艳红艳红的
贴在高耸的脚手架旁
泪眼　闪出远方老家媳妇头上的那朵花

## Sunset (II)

*So brightly red*
*Sticking beside the towering scaffolding*
*Flashing in tearful eyes, the flower on his wife's head far in his*
*hometown*

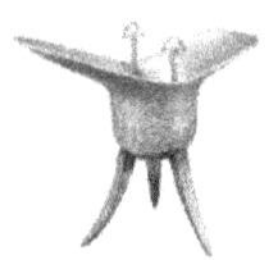

# ~*240*~

## 夕阳（三）

那么火红，那么旺盛
一群海鸥扇着翅膀　叽叽喳喳
争相阻止它下沉

### Sunset (III)

*So fiery red, so vibrant*
*A flock of seagulls flap their wings, clamoring*
*Rushing to halt its sinking*

# ~241~

# 溪水

洋洋自得地流淌着
流到大海
顿时不再作声

**Brook Water**

*Gurgling along contentedly*
*It flows into the sea*
*And suddenly falls silent*

# ~242~

# 溪边柳

今生不能投怀你的激流
但定要为你守候家园
等你凯歌归来

## *The Willow by the Brook*

*Though I can't merge with your rushing tides in this life*
*I will stand guard by your home*
*Patiently awaiting your triumphant return*

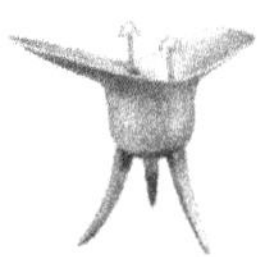

# ~243~

# 夏

臭脾气
热络时　热得你面红耳赤
说翻脸　马上就乌云密布

## **Summer**

*Stinking Temper*
*When affectionately warm, it blushes you*
*When relations sour, clouds gather, a storm looms*

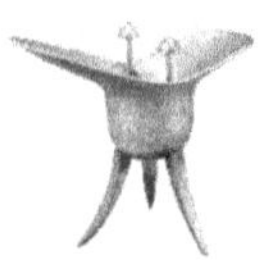

# ~244~

## 夏末秋初

青蛙、秋蝉、蟋蟀窃窃私语
为如何拓展晚夏的美
决定唱出一个秋高气爽


### Late Summer and Early Autumn

*Frogs, cicadas, and crickets whisper*
*Discussing how to enhance late summer's allure*
*They decide to sing of an invigorating autumn*

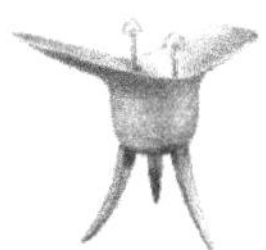

# ~245~

# 下海

哪里有潮
哪里难免
此起彼伏

## **Venturing into the Sea**

*Where tides exist
There the inevitability of
Rising and falling*

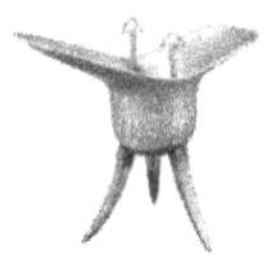

# ~246~

# 下雨了（一）

父亲撑起了伞
伞下是我
雨中是他

## Raining (I)

*Father holds the umbrella*
*Under it I stand*
*In the rain he stands*

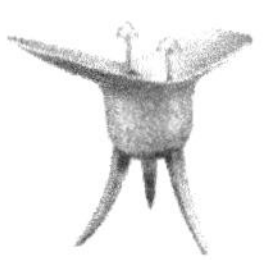

# ~247~

## 下雨了（二）

那老农跪在地上
仰天
捧起双手

### Raining (II)

*The old farmer, on bended knees*
*Raises his cupped hands*
*Toward the sky*

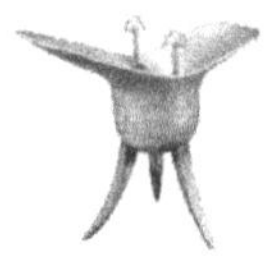



# 鲜嫩的荔枝

哪一只
不是通过枯瘦的虬枝
汲取养分

## *Tender Lychee Fruits*

*Which one among them*
*Doesn't draw sustenance*
*From the withered, sinuous branches*

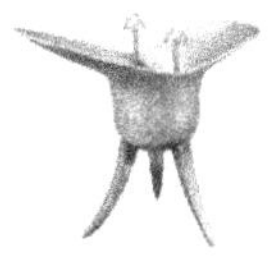



# 乡暮

夕阳剪影山坡
牧童骑牛悠然而下
笛声　轻抚十万感激摇迎的黄金穗

## The Countryside Dusk

*The sunset silhouettes hillside*
*The boy rides his cow, descending leisurely*
*The flute's melody caresses the golden rice ears, that sway in grateful*
*welcome*

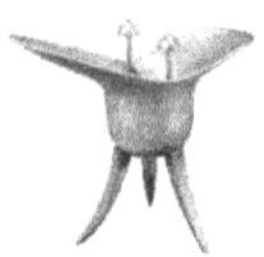

# ~250~

# 心头

笼罩着一朵
年轻时丢失的
——云

## *My Heart*

*Is Enshrouded*
*By a cloud*
*Lost in the days of youth*

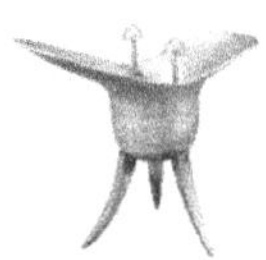

# ~251~

# 小巷

深深，向着落日的石格路*
斑驳着童年的记忆
萦绕着出不去

## The Alley

*Deep, towards the shattered granite path facing the setting sun*
*Flecked with the mottled memories of childhood*
*Lingering, unable to escape*

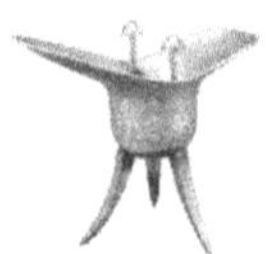

# ~252~

# 小草

风过处
槐树大哥倒了
它为什么仍然挺立着

## *Grass*

*A gust blows by*
*The locust tree falls*
*Why does the grass still stand upright*

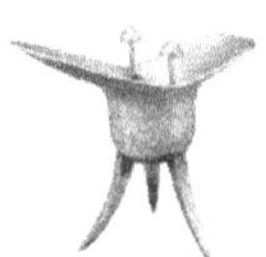

# ~*253*~

# 小村一隅

一支红杏漫出墙来
一只蝴蝶缠着不走
谁之过

## *The Village Corner*

*A red apricot branch crawls over the wall*
*A butterfly frolics over it and won't leave*
*Whose fault is it?*

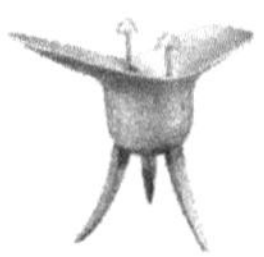

# ~254~

# 校花

平静夜空里的闪电
到哪
哪里风雨交加


## *Campus Beauty*

*Lightning in the peaceful night sky*
*Wherever she goes*
*There, quickly storms brew*

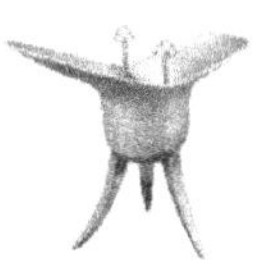

# ~255~

箫

直述
愁
肠

## Xiao*

*Straightly airs*
*The sorrow*
*Of the heart*

*Note   While the Chinese musical instrument Di (笛子, dí zi) is held horizontally, Xiao (箫, xiāo) vertically.*

# ~256~

## 心

乱得象树杈
梢尖遥望牛郎织女星
不见鹊桥

## *Heart*

*Disarrayed as tree forks*
*Branch tips gaze afar at Altair and Vega*
*Yet fail to see the Magpie Bridge*

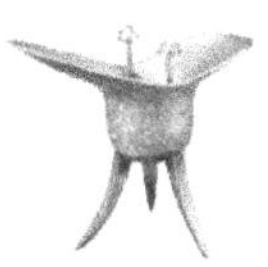

# ~257~

## 心窝里酿的酒

不需鼎
装入爵
醇厚、回味，飘香悠远

### The Wine Brewed in My Heart

*Needs no cauldron*
*Held in a goblet*
*Drifting afar with richness, aftertaste, and fragrance*

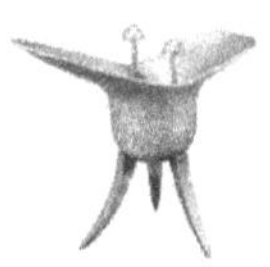

# ~258~

## 汹涌的乌云间

一条被脚铐数千年的古松
腾龙舞爪地——
欲飞

### Amidst the Billowing Dark Clouds

*An ancient pine, shackled for millennia*
*Rears like a dragon, clawing and leaping——*
*Yearning to soar*

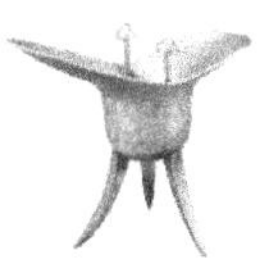

# ~259~

# 雪莲（一）

孤傲地绽放在雪山上
是因为那里远离尘世
还是与天咫尺

## Snow Lotus (I)

*Blooms with solitary pride on the snow mountain ——*
*Is it because it is far from the mortal world*
*Or because it is close to the heavens?*

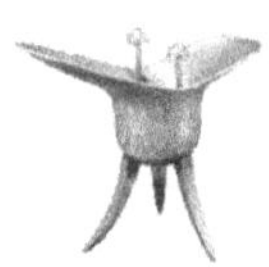

# ~260~

# 雪莲（二）

宁可隐身于寒冷的冰雪峰巅
也不苟且在舒适的温柔乡野
难道是因为那里咫尺九霄

## *The Snow Lotus (II)*

*Rather to conceal amidst the cold, icy peaks*
*Than compromise in the comfortable and gentle countryside*
*Is it because that place is within reach of the vast sky*

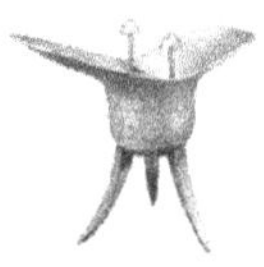

# ~261~

# 雪，丹青高手

几枝淡桠外
茫茫的留白，延至远方的起伏
数点檐形冒着炊烟

## Snow, Master of Ink and Wash

*Beyond a few faint branches*
*Stretches vast emptiness, extending to the undulating horizon*
*From a few eaves curves up wisps of smoke*

# ~262~

## 雪花

穿过漫漫长空
有的落在沟壑里，有的落在田野上
他飘上一朵梅花，结成了晶莹

### *Snowflakes*

*Through the vast sky*
*Some fall into ravines, some onto fields*
*He drifts onto a plum blossom, forming into a clear crystal*

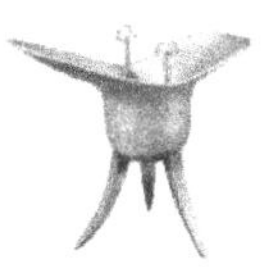

# ~263~

## 驯马师

无需缰绳马鞭
两根银弦　一束马尾
万马奔腾　排山倒海

## *Horse Tamer*

*No need for reins or whips*
*Two silver strings, a bundle of horse's tail*
*Thousands of steeds surge in sweeping momentum*

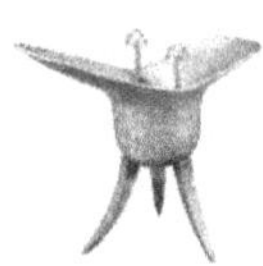

# ~264~

# 烟（一）

黑夜里一个烧红的窟窿
吧嗒吧嗒，每一吸
都直达心头的痛


## *The Cigarette (I)*

*A burning red hole in the dark night*
*Crackle, crackle, every inhale*
*Reaches straight the ache in the heart*

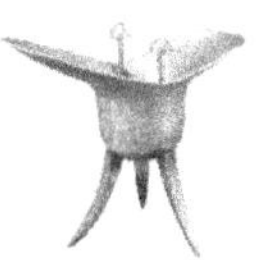

# ~265~

# 烟（二）

一根消愁管
越吸
愁越愁

## The Cigarette (II)

*A pipe to dispel sorrow*
*The more one draws*
*The deeper the sorrow*

# ~266~

# 烟（三）

吸进去，吐出来
是你驾着它神游
还是它享受着在你神经里蛰伏


## The Cigarette (III)

*Inhale, exhale*
*Do you steer it on an ecstatic voyage*
*Or does it enjoy lurking in your nerves?*

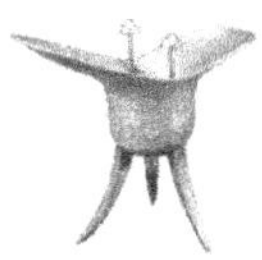

# ~267~

# 阳光下

渐干的露珠
为折射着偌大世界
满面泛光

## Under the Sunlight

*The drying dewdrop*
*Shimmers with a radiant glow on its face*
*As it reflects the vast world*

# ~268~

## 摇摆

东边太阳初升
西边月亮未落
中间的草左顾右盼

## *Sway*

*The sun rises in the east*
*The moon has yet to set in the west*
*In between, the grass looks left and right*

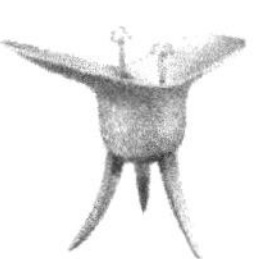

# ~269~

# 野花

在荒山
却总是笑容灿烂地
等风把它们的子孙送往远方

## *Wildflowers*

*Amidst the barren mountains*
*They always smile brightly*
*Awaiting the wind to carry their descendants afar*

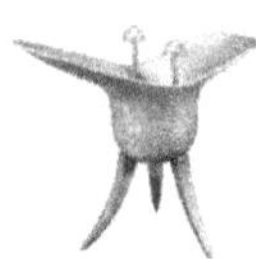

# ~270~

# 夜空（一）

星罗棋布
谁是
执子之手

## Night Sky (I)

*Starry chessboard*
*Whose hand is*
*Holding the pieces?*

# *~271~*

# 夜空（二）

一只孤雁
横过满月
破镜望重圆

## ***Night Sky (II)***

*A lonely goose*
*Crosses the full moon*
*Yearning to restore the broken mirror*

# ~272~

## 夜色静谧

月在云里走
云在湖中游
湖在你我心窗里涟漪

### The Night Is Peaceful

*The moon roams through the clouds*
*The clouds drift upon the lake*
*The lake ripples in the window of our hearts*

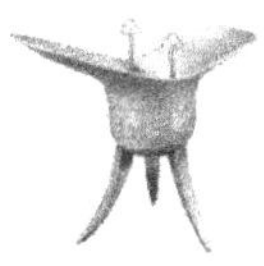

# ~273~

易

黑对白　白对黑

嘴对尾　尾对嘴

我眼中有你　你眼中有我　追逐不息

## Change*

*Black opposes white, white opposes black*
*Mouth faces tail, tail faces mouth*
*In my eye, there is you; in your eye, there is me, chasing endlessly*

Note: 易 (Yì) in the Book of Changes refers to transformation and the constant flow of opposites, symbolized by the Yin-Yang diagram. It reflects balance, harmony, and adaptability to life's cyclical changes.

# ~274~

一声夯号

喊出诗经、楚辞、十九首
唐诗、宋词、新诗
还有今天的三行

## A Ram's Call

*Inspired the 'Book of Songs', 'Chu Ci', and 'Nineteen Old Poems'*
*Tang poems, Song verses, modern poetry*
*And today's three-line verses*

*Note: This three lines trace the evolution of Chinese poetry: from the Shijing (Book of Songs) and Chuci (Songs of the Chu), to the poetic masterpieces of the Tang and Song dynasties, and up to modern three-line poetry, showcasing the rich, diverse history and development of Chinese poetic forms.*

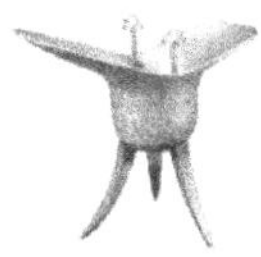

# ~275~

# 一声雁鸣

擦过高空建筑工的耳际
叩开了通往他老家的心门
屋里，媳妇还在月子里

## A Call of a Goose

*Brushes past the ear of the high-rise worker*
*Knocking on his heart's door to the home in his hometown*
*Inside, his wife is still in her confinement*

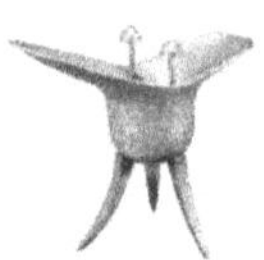

# ~276~

# 一只羊

站在贫瘠的峭壁上
瞭望边界墙那边的
肥沃草原

## The Goat

*Standing on the barren cliff*
*Gazes beyond the border wall*
*To the lush grasslands*

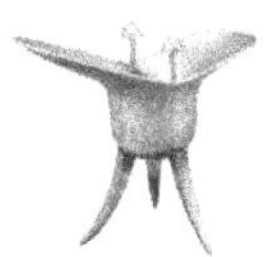

# ~277~

# 衣板

母亲搓塌的木棱
去了哪里
——她的那根拐棍?

## *The Washboard*

*Where have the ridges mother rubbed flat*
*Gone to*
*— Her walking stick?*

# ~278~

# 忆江南

长
相
思

## *Recalling the South*

*Evokes*
*Enduring*
*Memories**

Note: Both the poem's title 忆江南 *(yì jiāng nán, Recalling the South)* and the content 长相思 *(cháng xiāng sī, Enduring Longing)* are names of classical Chinese poetic forms.

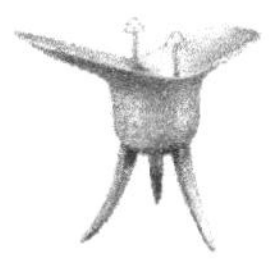



# 鹰

没有丈天量地的胸怀
岂能上天戏云
入海衔鱼?

## *The Eagle*

*Without a vast heart spanning heaven and earth*
*Could it soar to toy with the clouds*
*And plunge into the sea to snatch fish?*

# ~280~

# 鹰与鸡

鹰影掠过草地
母鸡急忙叼起小虫
钻进草丛

## The Eagle and the Hen

*The shadow of an eagle skims the grassy field*
*A hen hurriedly snatches a small insect*
*Vanishing into the thicket*

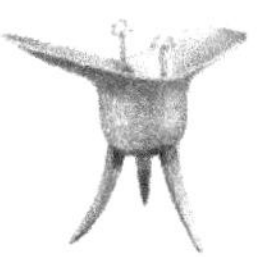

# ~281~

## 元宵

被搓得无论多圆润
未经江湖的沸煮
总上不了台面

### Tangyuan Dumpling

*No matter how perfectly rounded*
*Without the bustling boil of the Jianghu world**
*It never makes it to the table*

Note: The Jianghu world comes from the Chinese expression 江湖 (ji āng hú, 'river and lake'), which metaphorically refers to society, the world of martial arts, and a realm of wandering, freedom, and adventure, among other things.

# ~*282*~

# 萤火虫

无边的黑色画布上
画着蓝色的
梦

## *Fireflies*

*Drawing blue*
*Dreams*
*On the boundless dark canvas*

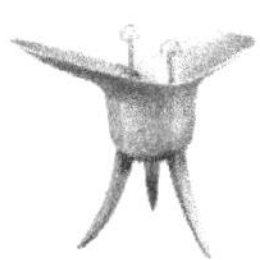

## ~283~

# 雨珠（一）

虽小
溅起的　是花
汇起的　是激流

## **Raindrops (I)**

*Though small*
*They splash as flowers*
*And gather as torrents*

# ~284~

# 雨珠（二）

没那千里舍身一跃
哪有
遍地生花

## *Raindrops (II)*

*Without sacrificing itself in a thousand-mile leap*
*How could there be*
*Blossoms everywhere*

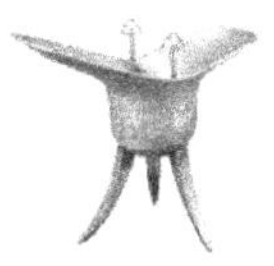

# ~285~

## 雨滴

在湖塘荡开无数涟漪
无数漪圈里倒映着无数拱桥
无数拱桥上无数对紧偎在伞下的身影

### *Raindrops*

*Spreading countless ripples across the pond*
*Which reflect countless arched bridges*
*Upon which, countless loving pairs huddle closely beneath
umbrellas*

# ~286~

# 雨后青柳

刚出浴的美人
曲尽朦胧
春意

## Post-Rain Green Willow

*A freshly bathed beauty*
*Each graceful curve unfurls*
*The misty spring's essence*

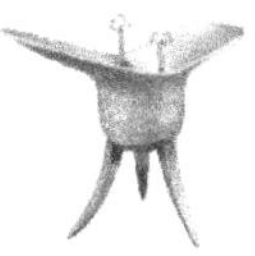

# ~287~

## 圆规

含天盖地
儒释道的祖师
中、无、空的前辈

### *A Compass*

*Encompassing heaven and earth*
*The Master of Confucianism, Daoism, and Buddhism**
*Predecessors of the Golden Mean, nothingness, and emptiness*

*Note: The 圆规 (compass) symbolizes the core philosophies of Confucianism, Buddhism, and Taoism. Confucianism emphasizes 中庸 (moderation), Buddhism focuses on 空 (emptiness), and Taoism on 无 (non-being), all concepts linked to the idea of zero or the circle, representing balance, void, and infinite potential.*

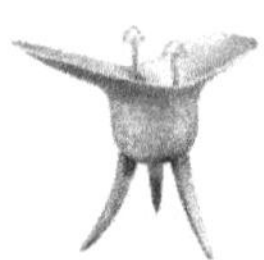

# ~288~

# 月（一）

云海里喷出的
夜明珠
寂静的夜晚，在多少人心里莹莹生辉

## The Moon (I)

*A Luminous Pearl*
*Emerges from the sea of clouds*
*Glowing in many hearts on tranquil nights*

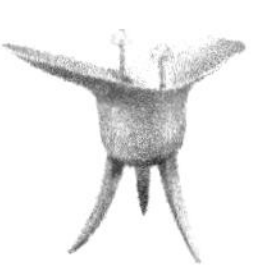

# ~*289*~

# 月（二）

一只荷包
里面装满
母亲给我讲过的童话故事

## The Moon (II)

*A rustic pouch*
*Brims with*
*The childhood tales Mother told me*

# ~290~

# 月牙

是只犀角
这边是我
那边是你


## The Crescent Moon

*A rhino horn*
*You on that side*
*And I, this*

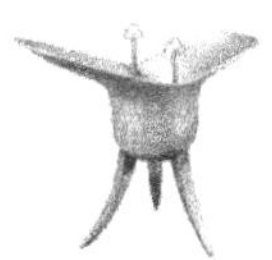

# ~291~

# 云（一）

出身沟壑
为升华不惜舍形毁容
终令万人仰视

## The Cloud (I)

*Born in the ravines*
*To ascend, it does not hesitate to forsake its form and destroy its*
*appearance*
*In the end, it makes millions look up in awe*

# ~292~

# 云（二）

蓝天里的万能拼图
美在随风而动的
一颗禅心

## The Cloud (II)

*A versatile puzzle in the blue expanse*
*What beautifies them is their Zen heart*
*That drifts with breeze*

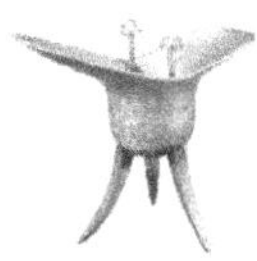

# ~293~

# 云（三）

坦对无常赋予的形
在蔚蓝的舞台上
尽展风姿

## The Cloud (III)

*Calmly facing the shapes that impermanence bestows,*
*They display their beauty*
*Upon the azure stage*

# *~294~*

## *云 (四)*

谁会吹
她就挽着谁走
难怪最后从天堂跌落沟壑

## **The Cloud (IV)**

*Whoever bluffs the best
She will take his arm and walk with him
No wonder she eventually falls from heaven into the gullies*

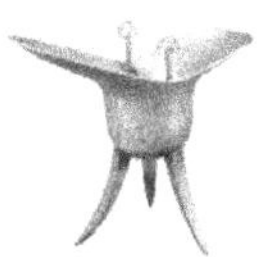

# ~295~

## 忠告

你成天让她呆在厨房
她怎能不让你
五味杂陈

### Sincere Advice

*You make her stay in the kitchen all the time*
*How could she not become*
*A blend of every flavor to you?*

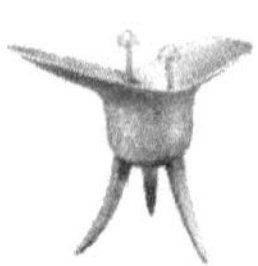

# ~296~

竹

没有始终紧绷的周身
怎能节节向上
挺入蓝天

## *Bamboo*

*Without tightening its body all the time*
*How can it rise segment by segment*
*Into the blue sky?*

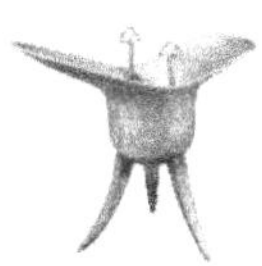

# ~297~

# 粽子（一）

飘的是香
还是"乡"
我有时真地分不清

## *Zongzi (I)*

*Drifting in the air*
*Is fragrance or "hometown*"*
*At times, I can hardly discern*

Note: In Chinese, the word "fragrance (香, xiāng)" and "hometown (乡, xiāng)" are homophones.

*~298~*

# 粽子（二）

裹着的
是掰不散的乡愁
牵丝带线　胶着粘稠

## *Zòngzi (II)*

*What is wrapped inside*
*Is an inseparable nostalgia*
*Binding, sticky, and thick*

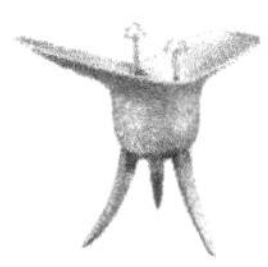

# ~299~

# 真有吗？

世上真有潘多拉魔盒吗？
如果没有
满车低头望着手上的是什么？

## *Does It Really Exist?*

*Does Pandora's box truly exist in this world?*
*If not*
*What are those in the car staring at in their hands?*

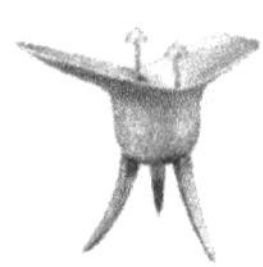



# 中秋之夜

抬头瞥见驾舟人回家
月美人腰下还湿漉着　就急急出浴
用粼粼裙褶牵引他

## Night of the Mid-Autumn Festival

*Seeing the boatman rowing home*
*The moon beauty rushes from her bath, still damp beneath her*
*waist*
*To guide him with her shimmering skirt folds*

# 作者与翻译

## 徐英才

　　大学教师、翻译家与诗人。在教育领域，他曾执教于中国复旦大学、加拿大麦克马斯特大学、美国德堡大学，课程涵盖古现代汉语、古现代中国文学、中国电影史、中国书法理论与实践、汉英英汉翻译理论与实践等多个领域。在翻译方面，他出版过许多译著，其中包括《英译唐宋八大家散文精选》《英译中国当代美文选》《英译中国经典散文选》《英译中国经典古诗词 100 首》《中国经典文化走向世界丛书散文卷三》《换言之》等等。他的译著有被当作国礼送往国外的，有被用作大学教材的。他的翻译原则是准确、传神、浑然。作为诗人，他出版了《徐英才诗选》《徐英才三行诗一百首》《江南诗意》等多部诗集。其诗歌理念是：语言朴实优美、诗意盎然形象，言自心声、言之有物，力求营造隽永的意境，努力让作品闪光。他的《中国三行诗理论与技巧》奠定了中国三行诗的理论基础，划清了中国三行诗与日本俳句以及汉俳的界限。他是华人诗学会的创办人与会长，汉英双语纸质诗刊《诗殿堂》的创办人与总编。

# Author and translator

## Xu Yingcai

A university professor, translator, and poet. In the field of education, he has taught at Fudan University in China, McMaster University in Canada, and DePaul University in the United States, covering courses in various areas such as Classical and Modern Chinese language, Classical and Modern Chinese Literature, History of Chinese Cinema, Chinese Calligraphy Theory and Practice, and Chinese-English and English-Chinese Translation Theory and Practice. As a translator, he has published many works, including "A Selection from the Eight Great Prose Masters of the Tang and Song Dynasties," "Selected Words of Contemporary Chinese Prose," "Selected Works of Classical Chinese Prose," "One Hundred Classic Chinese Poems," "Chinese Classic Culture Going Global Series: Essays Volume Three," and "In Other Words," and more. His translations have been given abroad as national gifts and used as university textbooks. His translation principles are "accuracy," "fidelity," and "coherence." As a poet, he has published collections such as "Selected Poems by Xu Yingcai," "One Hundred Three-Line Poems by Xu Yingcai," "Poetic Sense of the South," and "Inspiration from Nature." His poetic philosophy emphasizes simple and beautiful language, vivid imagery, expressing the heart's voice, and meaningful content. He strives to create lasting artistic concepts and to make his work shine. His "Chinese Three-Line Poetry Theory and Techniques" established the theoretical foundation of Chinese three-line poetry and clarified the distinctions between Chinese three-line poetry, Japanese haiku, and Chinese haiku. He is the founder and president of the Chinese Poetry Association, as well as the founder and chief editor of the bilingual Chinese-English poetry journal Poetry Hall.

www.ingramcontent.com/pod-product-compliance
Lightning Source LLC
Chambersburg PA
CBHW070408310726
48977CB00003B/605